For the executive, a *Shirt and Tie* cake.

Cowboys young and old will get a kick out of a plaid *Cowboy Shirt* cake, complete with western string tie.

Like the oxford shirt, this *Father's Day Shirt* cake is appropriate for most any occasion.

Better Homes and Gardens®

CREATIVE Cake Decorating

BETTER HOMES AND GARDENS® BOOKS

Editor: Gerald M. Knox
Art Director: Ernest Shelton
Managing Editor: David A. Kirchner

Food and Nutrition Editor: Doris Eby
Department Head—Cook Books: Sharyl Heiken
Senior Food Editors: Rosemary C. Hutchinson,
    Elizabeth Woolever
Senior Associate Food Editor: Sandra Granseth
Associate Food Editors: Jill Burmeister, Linda Foley,
    Linda Henry, Julia Malloy, Alethea Sparks, Marcia Stanley,
    Diane Yanney
Recipe Development Editor: Marion Viall
Test Kitchen Director: Sharon Stilwell
Test Kitchen Home Economists: Jean Brekke, Kay Cargill,
    Marilyn Cornelius, Maryellyn Krantz, Marge Steenson

Associate Art Directors: Linda Ford, Neoma Alt West,
    Randy Yontz
Copy and Production Editors: Marsha Jahns,
    Nancy Nowiszewski, Mary Helen Schiltz, David A. Walsh
Assistant Art Directors: Harijs Priekulis, Tom Wegner
Senior Graphic Designers: Alisann Dixon, Linda Haupert,
    Lyne Neymeyer
Graphic Designers: Mike Burns, Mike Eagleton, Deb Miner,
    Stan Sams, D. Greg Thompson, Darla Whipple,
    Paul Zimmerman

Editor in Chief: Neil Kuehnl
Group Editorial Services Director: Duane L. Gregg

General Manager: Fred Stines
Director of Publishing: Robert B. Nelson
Director of Retail Marketing: Jamie Martin
Director of Direct Marketing: Arthur Heydendael

CREATIVE CAKE DECORATING

Editor: Jill Burmeister
Copy and Production Editor: Mary Helen Schiltz
Graphic Designer: Deb Miner
Consultant: Jill Mead
Photographer: Mike Dieter
Illustrations: Thomas Rosborough

Our seal assures you that every recipe in *Creative Cake Decorating* has been tested in the Better Homes and Gardens® Test Kitchen. This means that each recipe is practical and reliable, and meets our high standards of taste appeal.

On the cover: *School Days Bus* (see recipe, page 29).

Contents

The Shape of Things to Come

If you think this is a book that shows you how to make frilly, fussy cakes (and then tries to tell you how easy it is), look again. These pages are filled with festive, fun-to-make cakes that are more creative than complicated. You'll enjoy putting together these cakes no matter how experienced you are. Our step-by-step instructions, along with pictures, tips, and diagrams, really do make creative cake decorating "a piece of cake".

The baking pans you'll need are found in most kitchens and are pictured on these two pages. We've kept the ingredients simple too. You can prepare most of the cakes with cake and frosting mixes or by using the recipes in the back of the book.

If you're unfamiliar with how to assemble, frost, and pipe frosting on a cake, get back to The Basics on page 82. Then try your hand at one of the clever cakes. With over 50 ideas to choose from, you're sure to find a cake that will rise to any occasion.

Football Field

2 cups creamy white frosting *(use Butter Frosting on page 88 or a creamy white frosting mix for a 2-layer cake)*
Green paste food coloring
1 15x10-inch baked Chocolate Cake *(see recipe, page 92)*

● Reserve 1 teaspoon of the creamy white frosting to make the football. Tint the remaining frosting with green food coloring. Frost sides and top of cake with green-tinted frosting.

---

3 *or* 6 breadsticks

● See picture and instructions at right for making two goal posts from the breadsticks.

● To mark yard lines, place a ruler along one long side of the cake and insert toothpicks in edge of cake 2, 3, 4, 5, 6, 7, 8, 9, 10, 11, and 12 inches from corner; repeat along opposite side of cake. Remove toothpicks, leaving marks in the frosting. Mark lines between toothpick marks by gently pressing the edge of a ruler or thin piece of cardboard into the frosting. To mark sidelines, place the ruler along one short side of the cake and insert toothpicks in edge of cake 2 inches from each corner; repeat on opposite side of cake. Mark lines between toothpicks with ruler or cardboard; remove toothpicks.

---

1 tube white decorator icing and plastic writing tip
Tubes of desired colors decorator icing

● With white decorator icing, retrace lines on cake. Add numbers at 50-yard line. Write team names at ends of cake with desired colors of decorator icing. Insert goal posts into cake at each end line. Fill in end zones with diagonal lines of white decorator icing.

Cut thin purchased breadsticks into six 3-inch lengths. For each goal post, insert half of a toothpick into the side of two breadstick pieces near the top. Attach to the crossbar by inserting the protruding toothpicks into the ends of a third breadstick piece.

---

1 teaspoon powdered sugar
¼ teaspoon unsweetened cocoa powder

● To make football, combine reserved frosting, the powdered sugar, and cocoa powder; knead till smooth. Shape into oval with pointed ends. Add stitching with white decorator icing; place on cake. Makes 12 to 15 servings.

Father's Day Shirt

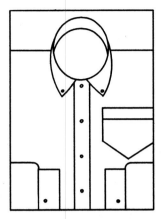

Batter for a 2-layer-size cake *(use a recipe on pages 90-92 or a 2-layer-size cake mix)*

● Pour batter into a greased and floured 13x9x2-inch baking pan and bake according to recipe directions. Cool in pan on a cooling rack.

2 cups creamy white frosting *(use Butter Frosting on page 88 or a creamy white frosting mix for a 2-layer cake)*
Paste food coloring

● Tint frosting with desired food coloring. Reserve ¼ cup of the frosting and tint darker for piping. Spread lighter frosting on top surface of cake in pan. Make the collar by building up and shaping the frosting.

Writing tip
Decorating bag *(see parchment cone on page 86 or use a pastry bag)*

● Use writing tip, decorating bag, and reserved dark frosting to outline the collar, shoulder seam, sleeves, pocket, and center placket of shirt (see diagram, top right).

Small gumdrops, sliced crosswise, *or* **candy-coated milk chocolate pieces**

● For buttons, place gumdrop slices or candy-coated milk chocolate pieces on center placket, cuffs, and collar. If desired, serve cake in a shirt box lined with tissue paper. Makes 12 servings.
Shirt and Tie: Prepare Father's Day Shirt as above, *except* omit buttons and reserve and tint only *2 tablespoons* of frosting a darker color; use to pipe outline on collar and shoulder seam only. Cut a tie shape from desired flavor(s) *rolled fruit leather* and place on cake.
Cowboy Shirt: Prepare Father's Day Shirt as above, *except* divide and tint frosting with *paste food coloring* as follows: tint ¾ cup with a dark color, 2 tablespoons with a contrasting dark color, and the remaining with a lighter complementary color. Spread the light-tinted frosting on top of cake. Form collar with about half of the ¾ cup dark-tinted frosting. Spread remaining dark-tinted frosting in 2-inch squares atop cake, making a checkered pattern. Pipe the 2 tablespoons contrasting frosting around collar and on shirt for yoke and center placket. For western tie, place a *shortbread cookie* at collar front and tuck ends of two 7-inch lengths of *shoestring licorice* under cookie.

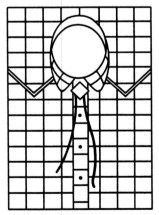

Build-a-House Cake

1 13x9-inch baked cake* *(use a recipe on pages 90-92 or a 2-layer-size cake mix)*

● Cut cake as shown in diagram below or opposite for desired house.

2 cups creamy white frosting* *(use Butter Frosting on page 88 or a creamy white frosting mix for a 2-layer cake)* **Paste food coloring (assorted colors)**

● Reserve ⅓ cup of the frosting for piping decorations on cake. Assemble the cut pieces of cake as shown in diagram, attaching the pieces with some of the remaining frosting. Let stand for 1 to 2 hours or till cut edges are slightly dry. Divide and tint remaining frosting with desired food coloring for roof and siding. Frost cake.

Writing tip
Decorating bag *(see parchment cone on page 86 or use a pastry bag)*
Assorted candies and cookies (optional)

● For windows and doors, tint reserved frosting with desired food coloring or leave untinted. Use writing tip and decorating bag to pipe windows and doors. If desired, add other decorations using assorted candies and cookies. Makes 12 servings.
***Note:** For A-frame house, use *two* 13x9-inch baked cakes. Assemble and frost using *4 cups* creamy white frosting. Makes 24 servings.

Build a house out of cake to welcome home the family wanderer, to give as a housewarming treat, or to celebrate the purchase of or the last mortgage payment on a new home.

After building one of the model homes, decorate it using "building materials" from your cupboard "tool shed". Try tinted frosting or pieces of licorice for windows and doors. Invert ice cream cones and cover them with green frosting leaves to make majestic evergreens. Or, use candies and cookies to trim the house or its landscape.

Basic house

One-story house with attached garage

Two-story house with attached garage

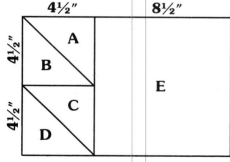

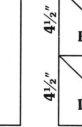

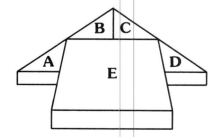

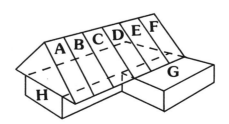

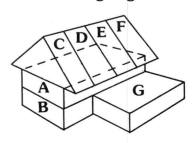

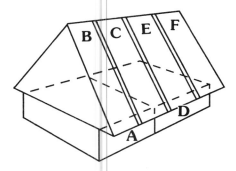

A-frame house

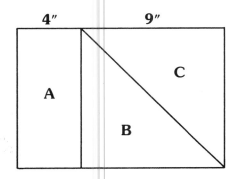

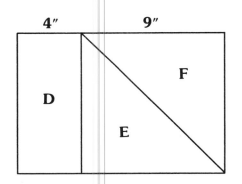

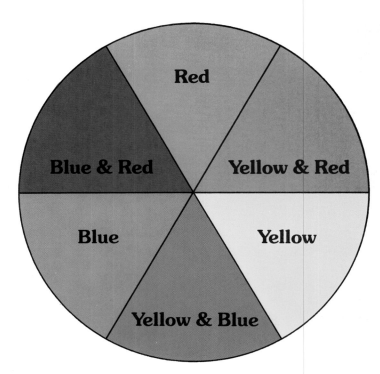

Color Wheel

By mixing the primary colors of red, yellow, and blue, you can tint frosting almost any color. (You'll need black paste food coloring, and plenty of it, to tint frosting black.) Use the color wheel above to determine what colors to mix. Always start out with small amounts of paste food coloring (as much as will fit on the tip of a toothpick) and add more as needed. To mix, first tint the frosting with the lighter color, then stir in the darker color, a tiny bit at a time, till the desired shade is reached. Because food colorings vary, you'll need to experiment to get just the shade you want.

Stained-Glass Cross

1 13x9-inch baked cake *(use a recipe on pages 90-92 or a 2-layer-size cake mix)*

● Cut the cake in half lengthwise. Cut 1 of the halves crosswise into thirds as shown in the diagram at right.

Royal Icing *(see recipe on page 89)*
Black paste food coloring

● Reserve about ⅓ cup of the icing; tint it black with black food coloring and keep covered. Spread some of the remaining untinted icing on one cut side of each of the three cake squares. Attach the frosted side of the cake squares to the cake strip as shown in diagram. Frost sides and top of the assembled cake with the remaining untinted icing.
  With a toothpick, draw flower petals, stems, and leaves in the icing. Draw random lines for stained-glass "leading". Let dry about 20 minutes.

Writing tip
Decorating bag *(see parchment cone on page 86 or use a pastry bag)*

● With writing tip, decorating bag, and reserved black-tinted frosting, retrace marks in icing and outline the top edge of the cake. Let icing dry 10 minutes.

About ¼ cup *each* mint-flavored jelly, apple jelly, grape jelly, and red currant jelly
About ½ cup apricot preserves

● Beat each type of jelly and preserves with a rotary beater till smooth; spoon into individual small bowls. Spoon some of the mint-flavored jelly into the outlined leaf portions. Spoon the apple, grape, and red currant jellies into separate petal portions of the flowers. Spoon apricot preserves into the remaining outlined portions. Let stand 1 hour before serving. Makes 12 servings.

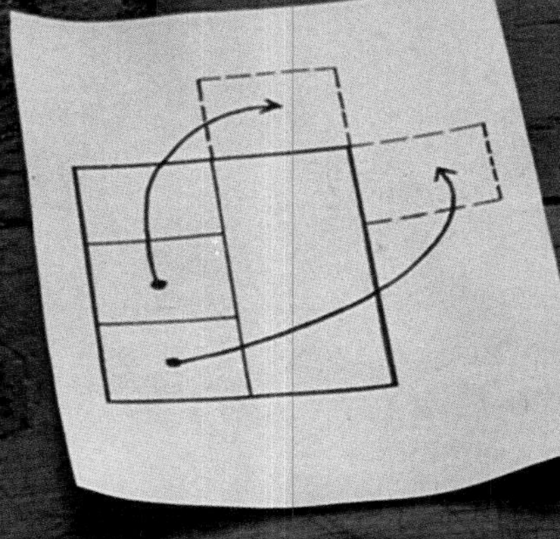

Stained-Glass Layer Cake: **Prepare *Stained-Glass Cross* as at left, *except* assemble and frost two 8-inch or 9-inch round cake layers with the untinted icing. Mark a circle with a toothpick 1 inch from cake edge. Mark petals, stems, and leaves inside the circle. Mark "leading" lines from points on the flower to the circle. Let dry 20 minutes. Retrace with the black-tinted icing. Let dry 10 minutes before spooning jellies and preserves into outlined portions.**

The Royal Icing used on this cake dries hard like candy and provides a firm base for the colorful jellies that give the cake its stained-glass effect.

STATE DRIVER LICENSE
Carl S. Newdriver
1234 Overdrive
Wheels, NE 54321

LICENSE NO.	RESTR. 1	TYPE 1
T002222	SEX	EXPIRES 9-15-86
ISSUED 9-15-83	M	BIRTHDAT 9-15-
HEIGHT 5' 10"	WEIGHT 155	

SIGNATURE
Carl S. Newdriver

POLYGLAS — F70-14

Driver's License

2 cups creamy white frosting *(use Butter Frosting on page 88 or a creamy white frosting mix for a 2-layer cake)*
1 13x9-inch baked cake *(use a recipe on pages 90-92 or a 2-layer-size cake mix)*

● Reserve ½ cup of the frosting for piping. Frost sides and top of the cake with the remaining frosting. With the long side of the cake facing you, place a ruler along the left side and insert toothpicks 1, 2, 2½, 3, 4, 5½, 7, and 8½ inches down from the top of cake; repeat along the right side of the cake. Remove toothpicks, leaving marks in frosting. Mark lines between toothpick marks by gently pressing the edge of a ruler or thin piece of cardboard into the frosting. Insert toothpicks in cake to mark area for the photograph.

Blue paste food coloring
Black paste food coloring
Writing tip
Decorating bag *(see parchment cone on page 86 or use a pastry bag)*

● Tint ⅓ cup of the reserved frosting with blue food coloring and the remaining with black food coloring. Use writing tip and decorating bag to pipe words and boxes as shown with blue-tinted frosting and information in boxes with black-tinted frosting.

Photograph

● To protect photograph, cover front and back with clear plastic wrap or cut waxed paper to fit and place behind photograph. Position photograph on cake. Makes 12 servings.

This *Driver's License* is the perfect birthday cake for a new driver. But you can easily adapt this design to resemble other sources of identification. For instance, turn it into a marriage license for the couple to be wed simply by varying the wording. Pattern the cake after a college or business ID card to celebrate collegiate life, a new job, or a promotion. Or, reconstruct an open passport for the overseas traveler.

Drawing Straight Lines on Cakes

Few of us can make perfectly straight lines freehand, especially while squeezing frosting out of a decorating bag. Here are some guidelines for making those frosting lines as straight as possible.

Place a ruler along one edge of the frosted cake. Insert toothpicks at the appropriate points. (All designs in this book requiring straight lines will specify the points to be marked.) Repeat measuring and marking with toothpicks on the opposite side of the cake. Before marking each line, remove the toothpicks; gently press the edge of a ruler or thin piece of cardboard into the frosting between the holes left by the toothpicks. Then, with a steady hand, pipe frosting over the lines.

1 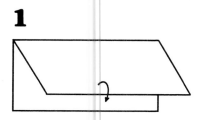 **2** 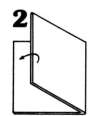 **3**  **4** 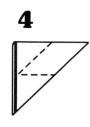 **5**

Country Quilt

2 cups creamy white frosting *(use Butter Frosting on page 88 or a creamy white frosting mix for a 2-layer cake)*
Paste food coloring
1 13x9-inch baked cake *(use a recipe on pages 90-92 or a 2-layer-size cake mix)*

● Reserve ½ cup of the frosting for decoration and border. Tint remaining frosting a light shade with food coloring; frost sides and top of cake with ¾ to 1 cup. Add more of the same coloring to the remaining lightly tinted frosting to make a darker shade. With the edge of a ruler or thin piece of cardboard, mark a line lengthwise down center of cake. Mark two lines across cake that divide the cake crosswise into thirds. (You will have 6 squares on the frosted cake.)

1 To make the pattern for the quilt design, first fold a 3½-inch square of waxed paper in half crosswise.

2 Fold in half crosswise again to make a small square.

3 Fold the square in half diagonally to make a right triangle.

4 With scissors, cut off two corners as shown, leaving corner with two folded edges uncut.

5 Unfold.

● Fold a 3½-inch square of waxed paper in half crosswise (step 1). Fold in half crosswise again to make a square (step 2). Fold in half diagonally to make a triangle (step 3). Leaving corner with two folded edges uncut, cut off the other two corners as shown (step 4). Open waxed paper. Place on one square of the frosted cake; with a toothpick, trace around the pattern. Repeat on remaining squares of cake.

Writing tip
Decorating bag *(see parchment cone on page 86 or use a pastry bag)*
Ribbon tip

● With a metal spatula or knife, spread dark-tinted frosting inside lines of design in each square.
Use writing tip and decorating bag to pipe 2 tablespoons of the reserved un-tinted frosting in "stitch lines" atop the darker designs and along the lines of each square.
Use ribbon tip and remaining untinted frosting to pipe a ruffled border around top edge of cake. (With the wide part of the ribbon tip on the edge of the cake and the narrow part off the cake edge, move the bag around the edge in a zigzag motion to ruffle the frosting.) Makes 12 servings.

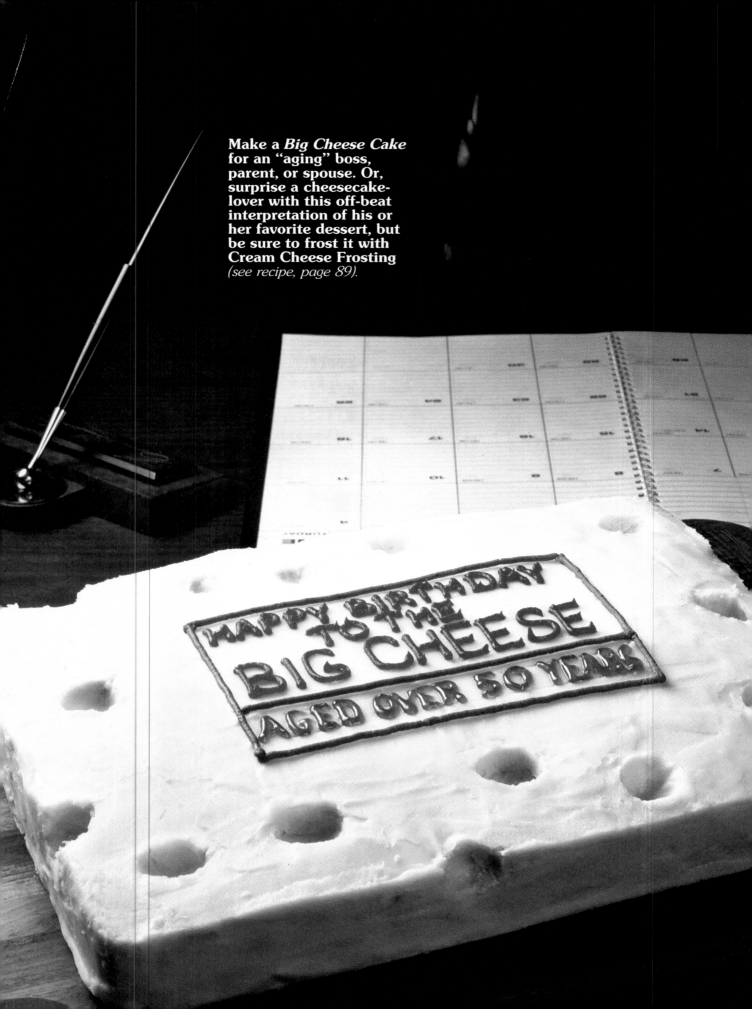

Make a *Big Cheese Cake* for an "aging" boss, parent, or spouse. Or, surprise a cheesecake-lover with this off-beat interpretation of his or her favorite dessert, but be sure to frost it with Cream Cheese Frosting *(see recipe, page 89).*

Big Cheese Cake

1 **13x9-inch baked cake** *(use a recipe on pages 90-92 or a 2-layer-size cake mix)*
2 **cups creamy white frosting** *(use Butter Frosting on page 88 or a creamy white frosting mix for a 2-layer cake)*

1 **tube blue decorator icing and plastic writing tip**
1 **tube red decorator icing**
1 **tube green glossy cake decorating gel**

● Cut a 6x4-inch rectangle from a piece of paper. Place atop cake in center. Insert toothpicks in cake at corners of rectangle to mark area for label. Set pattern aside. With a melon ball cutter or a sharp knife, cut holes in cake in various places outside rectangle. Remove toothpicks. Frost sides and top of cake, spreading frosting deep into holes.

● Gently place pattern atop frosting in center of cake and trace around it with a toothpick. With blue decorator icing and writing tip, retrace lines of rectangle. Make a line across rectangle about 1½ inches from bottom. With red decorator icing write message above line. With green gel, write message below line. Makes 12 servings.

Use a melon ball cutter or a sharp knife to cut holes in various places on the cake, avoiding the 6x4-inch rectangle marked off for the label. Make the holes about 1 inch deep so that when you spread frosting into the holes, the depressions will be noticeable.

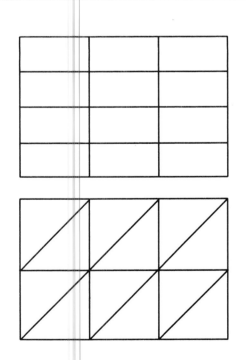
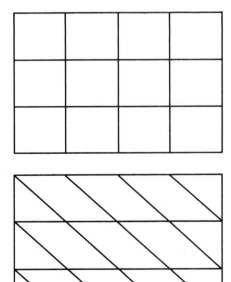

Cutting 13x9-inch Cakes

Show your creativity not only in how you decorate a cake but also in how you serve it. Use these patterns to cut cakes into rectangles, squares, triangles, or diamonds—whatever shape suits your fancy. Each pattern makes 12 servings.

Gumball Machine
(see recipe, page 24)

Cookie Cutter Cake
(see recipe, page 25)

Coloring Book Cake *(see recipe, page 22)*

Candy Land Express *(see recipe, page 23)*

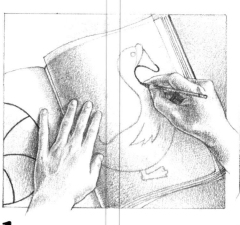

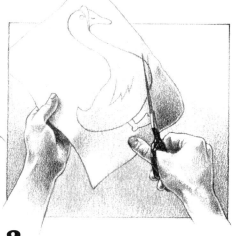

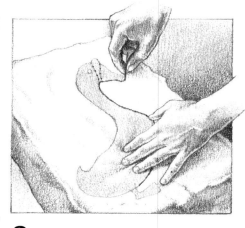

1

2

3

Coloring Book Cake

Pictured on page 21—

1 13x9-inch baked cake *(use a recipe on pages 90-92 or a 2-layer-size cake mix)*
2 cups creamy white frosting *(use Butter Frosting on page 88 or a creamy white frosting mix for a 2-layer cake)*

● Frost the sides and top of the cake with the creamy white frosting. (Or, leave cake in pan and frost top only.) Let the frosted cake stand about 1 hour or till the frosting is slightly firm.

1 To transfer the picture, place a piece of waxed paper over the coloring book page. With a pencil, trace over the outline and simple details of the picture so you can see the image on the waxed paper.

Coloring book page

● Meanwhile, place waxed paper over coloring book page and trace outline and simple details on the waxed paper with a pencil. Cut out figure from waxed paper.

2 Use scissors to cut the picture out of the waxed paper. Center the cutout on the frosted cake.

● To transfer design to cake, position waxed-paper cutout on cake. With a toothpick, trace around cutout. Transfer simple details by poking holes through markings on waxed paper with a toothpick. Lift off waxed paper.

3 With a toothpick, trace around the cutout. To transfer the details of the picture to the cake, poke the toothpick through the markings on the waxed paper at close intervals to make dotted lines in the frosting underneath.

Tubes of decorator icing (assorted colors) and plastic tips
Assorted colors of glossy cake decorating gel

● Using appropriate colors of decorator icing and cake decorating gel, retrace design marked in frosting. Then squeeze the tube of icing or gel inside outlines, using straight lines, till the entire design is colored in. (If desired color gel is not available, use the color wheel on page 11 to mix the gel colors; spread with a metal spatula or knife.) Serves 12.

Candy Land Express

Pictured, pages 20 and 21—

1 **13x9-inch baked Chocolate Cake** *(see recipe, page 92)*
2 **cups creamy chocolate frosting** *(use Chocolate Butter Frosting on page 88 or a creamy milk chocolate frosting mix for a 2-layer cake)*

● Cut cake according to directions and as shown in diagram at right. To make frosting the cake easier, let the cut cake stand 1 to 2 hours or till cut edges of cake are slightly dry.

Frost sides and top of each piece of cake with the chocolate frosting. For engine and caboose, attach each of the smaller pieces of cake to a larger piece as shown at right, smoothing adjoining areas with more frosting.

Assorted candy and cookie decorations
1 **tube yellow decorator icing and plastic tip**

● With assorted candies and cookies, decorate sides and tops of frosted cake pieces using a different decoration for each. Attach round candies to sides of cake pieces for wheels. Make windows on sides of engine and caboose with yellow decorator icing. If desired, make train track using chocolate caramel logs and shoestring licorice. Serves 12.

To cut the cake into cars, first cut the cake in half lengthwise. Then cut the cake crosswise into six equal rows to form 12 rectangles. Cut one of these rectangles in half crosswise. Because soft cake edges are difficult to frost, let the cut cake stand for 1 to 2 hours so the edges dry slightly before frosting.

To assemble the engine, attach one of the small cake squares atop the end of one rectangle. For the caboose, attach the other small cake square atop the center of another rectangle. Use a little bit of frosting to smooth the areas where the pieces of cake join.

Here are some things you might want to have on hand for "workin' on the railroad":
1 Cinnamon-flavored oblong candies
2 Striped round peppermint candies
3 Chocolate caramel logs
4 Candy corn
5 Fruit-flavored circle candies
6 Gumdrops
7 Animal crackers
8 Nuts
9 Chewy fruit-flavored squares
10 Shoestring licorice
11 Bite-size shredded corn squares
12 Tiny marshmallows
13 Candy-coated milk chocolate pieces
14 Red cinnamon candies
15 Caramel pinwheels

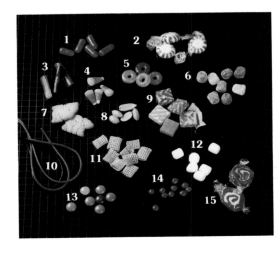

Gumball Machine

Pictured on page 20— ·

---

2 cups creamy white frosting *(use Butter Frosting on page 88 or a creamy white frosting mix for a 2-layer cake)*
Green paste food coloring
1 tablespoon unsweetened cocoa powder

● Divide and tint the creamy white frosting as follows: tint ¾ cup green with green food coloring, tint ½ cup brown with the unsweetened cocoa powder, and leave remaining ¾ cup untinted.

Make the background frosting for this cake any color you like. Create exciting colors by mixing together paste food colorings, using the color wheel on page 11 as a guide. To make the frosting olive green, we first tinted it with green paste food coloring. Then we added just a touch of red and a touch of yellow and mixed thoroughly.

---

1 13x9-inch baked cake *(use a recipe on pages 90-92 or a 2-layer-size cake mix)*

● Place a 7-inch paper plate atop cake slightly toward one end. Insert toothpicks around plate; remove plate. Outline the gumball machine base with toothpicks. Frost sides and top of cake outside toothpicks with the green-tinted frosting. Spread ½ cup of the untinted frosting inside circle of toothpicks. Spread chocolate frosting inside toothpicks outlining the base. Remove toothpicks.

Writing tip
Decorating bag *(see parchment cone on page 86 or use a pastry bag)*
Candy-coated milk chocolate pieces

● Use writing tip and decorating bag to pipe remaining untinted frosting for outline and details of gumball machine. Press candies atop circle of untinted frosting. Makes 12 servings.

Before you frost the cake, mark off the area for the gumball machine. For the "glass" ball, invert a 7-inch paper plate atop the cake slightly toward one end. Insert toothpicks around the edge of the plate; remove the plate. For the base of the machine, also outline a boxlike area with toothpicks. Now frost the cake according to the recipe directions.

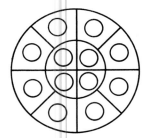

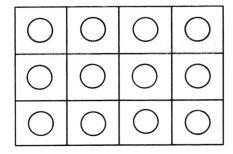

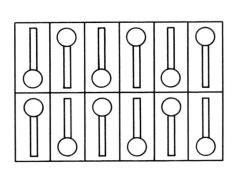

Here are some different ways you can "stamp" the top of a frosted cake with a cookie cutter so that each piece has a design. In choosing the size of cookie cutter to use and in planning the pattern on the cake, remember that a 2-layer-size cake should make 12 servings.

Cookie Cutter Cake *Pictured, pages 20 and 21—*

3 cups creamy white frosting *(use Butter Frosting on page 88 or a creamy white frosting mix for a 2-layer cake)*
Paste food coloring (assorted colors)
1 13x9-inch baked cake *or* two 8- *or* 9-inch round baked cake layers *(use a recipe on pages 90-92 or a 2-layer-size cake mix)*

● Tint 2 cups of the creamy white frosting with one color of paste food coloring. Divide and tint the remaining 1 cup of frosting as desired with assorted food colorings. (If using a creamy white frosting mix, refrigerate or freeze any unused frosting.) Frost sides and top of the large cake (or assemble and frost sides and top of cake layers) with the 2 cups tinted frosting.

Cookie cutter
Writing tip *or* star tip
Decorating bag *(see parchment cone on page 86 or use a pastry bag)*
Miniature semisweet chocolate pieces, chopped nuts, *or* small candies (optional)

● Gently press cookie cutter into frosting at equal intervals to make 12 impressions, dipping cookie cutter in hot water and shaking off excess water after each pressing. Using desired tip and decorating bag, retrace and fill in the cookie cutter outline with the assorted colors of frosting. If desired, decorate with miniature chocolate pieces, nuts, or candies. To serve, cut between individual designs. Makes 12 servings.

Got-Your-Number Cake

1 13x9-inch baked cake *(use a recipe on pages 90-92 or a 2-layer-size cake mix)*
3 cups creamy white frosting *(use Butter Frosting on page 88 or 2 creamy white frosting mixes for a 2-layer cake)*

● Refer to diagrams opposite to cut cake for desired number. To make the cake easier to frost, let cut pieces of cake stand 1 to 2 hours or till cut edges are slightly dry. Assemble pieces, using some of the frosting to secure them.

Paste food coloring

● Reserve ½ cup of the creamy white frosting. Tint the remaining frosting with desired paste food coloring. (If using frosting mix, refrigerate or freeze any unused frosting.) Frost all sides and top of the cake with the tinted frosting.

Star tip
Decorating bag *(see parchment cone on page 88 or use a pastry bag)*
Red cinnamon candies

● With a toothpick, draw lines atop cake to mark serving portions in frosting. Using star tip and decorating bag, pipe reserved untinted frosting in individual stars around top edge of cake and over serving portion marks. Pipe a star of frosting in the center of each portion. Gently press a cinnamon candy atop each center star. Makes 8 to 12 servings.

The grid at right shows you how to cut and piece the cake to make the number you want. The dark shaded areas on the grid represent leftover portions of cake. If you're using yellow or white cake, save the trimmings to make a luscious dessert called trifle.

Assemble a trifle in a few easy steps. First spread the cake trimmings with jam or jelly and place in a bowl. Now sprinkle them with sherry, brandy, or rum. Finally top with your favorite fruit, custard, and whipped cream.

1 square measures about 3 inches.

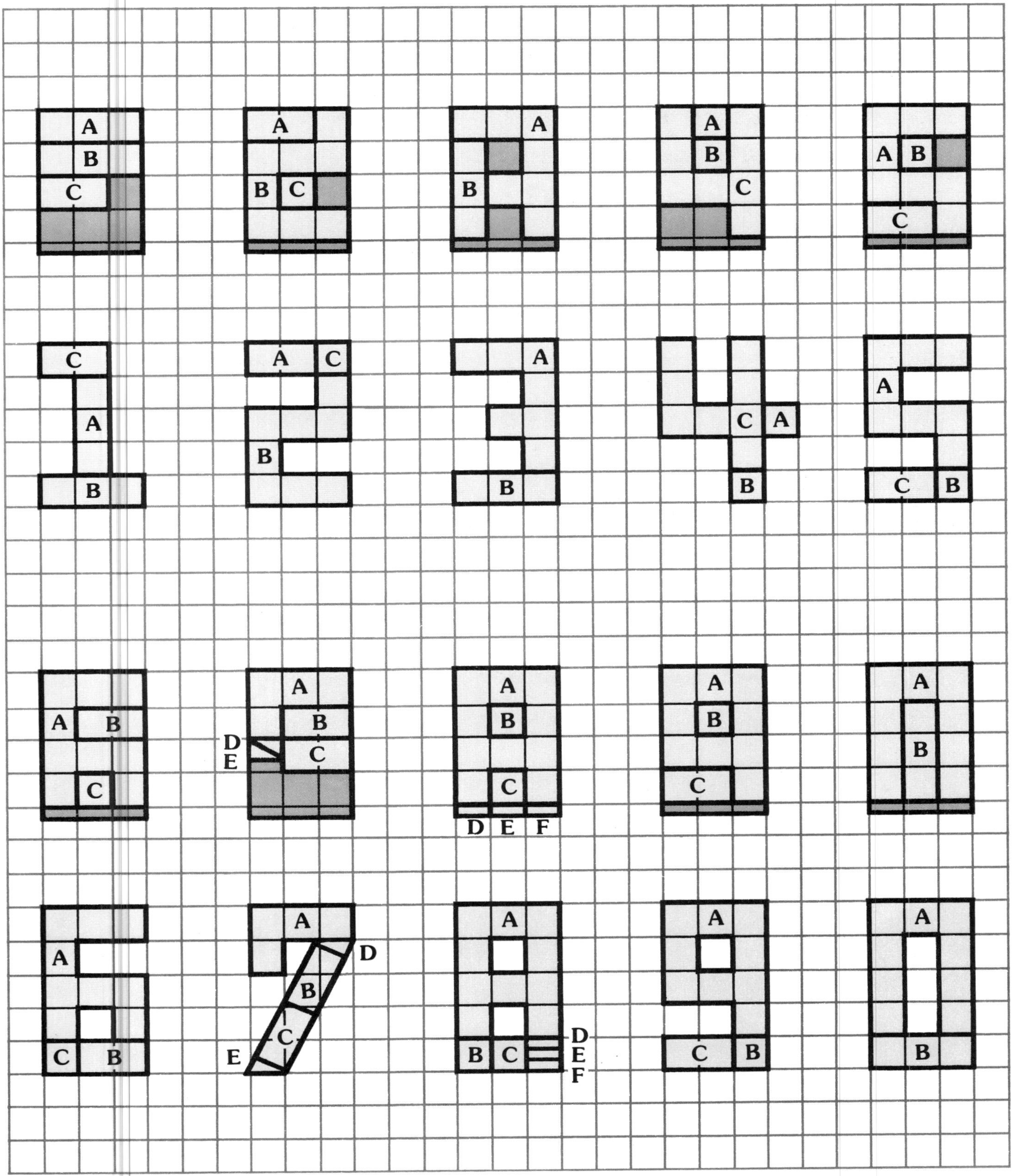
A
B
C
A
B C
A
B
A
B
C
A B
C
C
A
B
A C
B
A
B
A
C
B
C A
B
A
C B
A B
C
A
B
D
E
C
A
B
C
D E F
A
B
C
A
B
A
C B
A
D
B
E
C
A
B C
D
E
F
A
C B
A
B

SCHOOL DAYS

Windows

Safety lights

Wheels

Bumpers

Grill

Turn signals

Headlights

Windshield and wipers

School Days Bus

Also pictured on the cover—

1 8-inch square baked cake *(use a recipe on pages 90-92 or a 1-layer-size cake mix)*

2 cups creamy white frosting *(use Butter Frosting on page 88 or a creamy white frosting mix for a 2-layer cake)*

● Cut the baked cake in half crosswise. Spread about 1/3 cup of the creamy white frosting over the top of one cake half. Top with the other cake half.

Red paste food coloring
Orange *or* **yellow paste food coloring**
1 cream-filled golden sponge cake

● Tint 2 tablespoons of the remaining frosting with red food coloring; set aside. Tint remaining frosting desired shade with orange or yellow food coloring; frost sides and top of the cake. Attach sponge cake to front and frost.

4 chocolate sandwich cookies *or* **jelly ring candies**
4 chocolate caramel logs
1 filled sugar wafer
4 to 6 sticks chewing gum
Black shoestring licorice
2 white circle candies
6 red cinnamon candies
2 small white oval mints
2 small orange oval mints
Writing tip
Decorating bag *(see parchment cone on page 86 or use a pastry bag)*

● Attach cookies or jelly ring candies for wheels. Attach chocolate caramel logs to front and back for bumpers. Place filled sugar wafer above front bumper for grill. Cut and attach gum for windows. Attach licorice to gum on front with some frosting for windshield wipers. Attach white circle candies for headlights, red cinnamon candies for safety lights, and small oval mints for turn signals.

Use writing tip, decorating bag, and red-tinted frosting to pipe words on sides and back of bus. Makes 8 servings.

Note: For a shortcut, use 2 frozen loaf pound cakes instead of an 8-inch square baked cake. Thaw the pound cakes; cut one in half lengthwise. Spread about 1/3 cup frosting atop the uncut pound cake. Top with one of the halves of the other pound cake. Continue as directed in recipe. (Use remaining pound cake half for another dessert.)

You don't have to be a mechanic to put together this *School Days Bus.* All of the parts are available at the grocery store.

If you'd rather build a city bus or a bus to send off or welcome back the cross-country traveler, omit the sponge cake on the front, "paint" the bus with blue or white frosting, and write the destination above the front windows.

To make these fruit baskets, start with one 8-inch square cake and cut it into four squares.

For each basket, stack *two* of the squares. Make the cakes wider at the top than at the bottom by slicing down each side at a slight angle.

Spread frosting between the layers of each cake. Then frost the sides and tops of the cakes.

Fruit Basket Duet

1 8-inch square baked cake (use a recipe on pages 90-92 or a 1-layer-size cake mix)	● Cut, stack, and trim cake according to instructions opposite. To make the cakes easier to frost, let cake stacks stand 1 to 2 hours or till cut edges are slightly dry.
1 teaspoon ground cinnamon **3 cups creamy white frosting** (use Butter Frosting on page 88 or a creamy white frosting mix for a 2-layer cake) **Basket-weave tip or leaf tip** **Decorating bag** (use parchment cone on page 86 or use a pastry bag)	● Stir cinnamon into 1¼ cups of the frosting; set aside. Use the remaining frosting to spread between layers and to frost sides and tops of cakes. (If using frosting mix, refrigerate or freeze any unused frosting.) Use basket-weave tip or leaf tip and decorating bag to pipe cinnamon frosting on cake sides in basket-weave design (see instructions at right).
2 cups fresh strawberries or fresh blueberries or 1 cup of each	● Arrange half of the fresh fruit atop each cake. Makes 2 cakes (8 servings).

For basket-weave design, first pipe a vertical strip of frosting on side of cake ½ inch from corner. Then make short horizontal strips long enough to go across it, leaving about ½ inch between each one. Make a second vertical strip close to the first and cross it with short horizontal strips that fit between those previously made. Continue around all sides. Finish with a continuous band around top for rim.

Box of Chocolates

1 8-inch square baked cake *(use a recipe on pages 90-92 or a 2-layer-size cake mix)*

1 cup creamy chocolate frosting *(use Chocolate Butter Frosting on page 88 or a creamy fudge frosting mix for a 1-layer cake)*

● Frost the sides and top of the cooled, baked cake with the 1 cup creamy chocolate frosting.

● Using a ruler as a guide, insert toothpicks in one top edge of cake about 1½ inches apart to make 5 equal segments. Repeat on remaining sides. Remove toothpicks. Mark lines between toothpick marks on opposite sides by gently pressing the edge of a ruler or thin piece of cardboard into the frosting.

1 tube white *or* pink decorator icing and plastic writing tip
Red candy heart
About 20 chocolate candies in paper cups

● Make letters with white or pink decorator icing and place the red candy heart on desired square. Place chocolate candies in paper cups atop the remaining squares. Makes 8 servings.

Think of the times you'd like to give someone a box of chocolates. Those are the times you could make a *Box of Chocolates* cake instead. Vary the phrase with the situation. "I Love You," "Get Well Soon," and "Thank You" are some fitting messages to write between the chocolates on the cake.

First-Class Parcel

1 cup creamy chocolate frosting *(use Chocolate Butter Frosting on page 88 or a creamy fudge frosting mix for a 1-layer cake)*

1 8-inch square baked cake *(use a recipe on pages 90-92 or a 1-layer-size cake mix)*

Black paste food coloring

1 tube white decorator icing and plastic writing tip

● Reserve 2 tablespoons of the chocolate frosting. Frost sides and top of cake with remaining frosting. Using a ruler as a guide, insert toothpicks in top edges of cake 1½ inches from each corner. Remove toothpicks. Mark 4 lines for string between toothpick marks on opposite sides of cake by gently pressing the edge of a ruler or thin piece of cardboard into the frosting.

● Tint reserved frosting black with black food coloring. Write address in center of cake; add mailing instructions. Make canceled stamp in upper right corner. With white decorator icing and writing tip, retrace lines for string, extending lines down sides of cake; make a bow at one point where lines intersect. Serves 8.

When someone you know is enduring finals, leaving on a trip, going to camp, or battling the blues, show them you care with a *First-Class Parcel* made with their favorite flavor of cake.

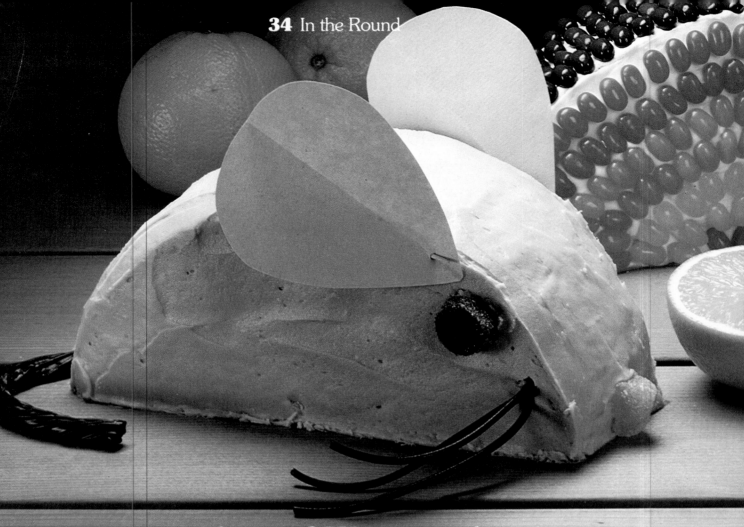

Slice of Watermelon

**1 8- *or* 9-inch round baked
cake layer** (use a recipe
on pages 90-92 or a 1-layer-
size cake mix)

**2 cups creamy white
frosting** (use Butter
Frosting on page 88 or a
creamy white frosting mix
for a 2-layer cake)

● To assemble the cake, cut the cake
layer in half crosswise. Spread about ¼
cup of the frosting on the large flat side
of one of the cake halves. Top with the
other half, flat side down. Place cake on
decorating surface, cut side away from
you. Slice ¼ inch off curved edge of
cake for a more stable cake.

**Red *or* pink paste food
coloring**
**Green paste food
coloring**

● Divide and tint remaining frosting as
follows: tint ¾ cup with red or pink food
coloring, tint ½ cup with green food
coloring, and leave ½ cup untinted.

**Miniature semisweet
chocolate pieces
or raisins**

● For rind, frost curved side of cake
with green-tinted frosting and spread a
½-inch band onto top curved edge and
across cut surface of cake. Repeat with
a ½-inch band of untinted frosting as
shown. Set cake upright on trimmed
edge; continue green and white bands
on other side. With red- or pink-tinted
frosting, frost rest of cake. Apply chocolate pieces or raisins to red area for
seeds. Makes 6 servings.

**All four of these
cakes are made
from round cake
layers that are cut
in half and
reassembled.
Pictured counter-
clockwise are *Slice
of Watermelon, Slice
of Orange, Pot-o'-
Gold Rainbow,* and
Mister Mouse (see
recipes, pages 36 and 37).**

Mister Mouse

Pictured on page 34—

1 **8- *or* 9-inch round baked
   cake layer** *(use a recipe on
   pages 90-92 or a 1-layer-
   size cake mix)*
2 **cups creamy white
   frosting** *(use Butter
   Frosting on page 88 or a
   creamy white frosting mix
   for a 2-layer cake)*

● To assemble the cake, cut the cake layer in half crosswise. Spread about ¼ cup of the frosting on the large flat side of one of the cake halves. Top with the other half, flat side down. Press layers together to secure. Place the cake, cut side down, on decorating surface or serving platter.

To put a curl in the tail of the mouse, place the licorice twist on a piece of foil in an oven set at 200° (or the lowest temperature) about 3 minutes or till softened. Remove and curl it into a circle. Hold it in place under a heavy book till cool.

Black paste food coloring

● Tint remaining frosting light gray with black paste food coloring. Frost all exposed surfaces of cake.

1 **large pink gumdrop**
1 **large black gumdrop**
1 **black licorice twist**
   **Black shoestring licorice,
   cut into 4-inch lengths**
   Pink construction paper

● Cut pink gumdrop in half from top to bottom; place one half at one end of cake for nose. Slice black gumdrop crosswise into 4 pieces. Place slices with flat sides on each side of the cake for eyes. Using licorice twist as a tail and shoestring licorice for whiskers, insert each into cake. Cut ears from construction paper in the shape of teardrops; crease in center. Just before serving, attach ears to cake with toothpicks. Makes 6 servings.

Pot-o'-Gold Rainbow

Pictured, pages 34 and 35—

1 **8- *or* 9-inch round baked cake layer** *(use a recipe on pages 90-92 or a 1-layer-size cake mix)*
2 **cups creamy white frosting** *(use Butter Frosting on page 88 or a creamy white frosting mix for a 2-layer cake)*

● To assemble the cake, cut the layer in half crosswise. Spread about ¼ cup of the frosting on the large flat side of one of the halves. Top with the other half, flat side down. Press layers together to secure. Place the cake, cut side down, on decorating surface or serving platter. Frost all exposed areas of cake with the remaining frosting.

Make a *Pot-o'-Gold Rainbow* to wish someone a promising future or to celebrate a goal fulfilled or dream come true.

Blue, red, orange, yellow, and green jelly beans

● Place blue jelly beans in rows to cover curved side of cake. With red jelly beans, make a border two rows wide on the flat sides of the cake, starting at the curved edge. Repeat with orange, yellow, and green jelly beans, making two-row bands with each color. Makes 6 servings.

Slice of Orange

Pictured on page 35—

1 **8- *or* 9-inch round baked cake layer** *(use a recipe on pages 90-92 or a 1-layer-size cake mix)*
2 **cups creamy white frosting** *(use Butter Frosting on page 88 or a creamy white frosting mix for a 2-layer cake)*

● To assemble the cake, cut the cake layer in half crosswise. Spread about ¼ cup of the frosting on the large flat side of one of the cake halves. Top with the other half, flat side down. Press layers together to secure. Place the cake, cut side down, on decorating surface or serving platter.

Change this cake into a lemon slice or lime slice by tinting the frosting shades of yellow or green instead of orange.

Orange paste food coloring

● Divide and tint remaining frosting with orange food coloring as follows: tint ¾ cup pale orange and 1 cup dark orange. Frost flat sides of cake with pale orange-tinted frosting. Frost curved side with about ½ cup of the dark orange-tinted frosting, spreading a ½-inch band onto both flat sides of cake. Mark sections of orange with a toothpick, leaving a small space between each section.

Star tip
Decorating bag *(see parchment cone on page 86 or use a pastry bag)*
Shelled sunflower nuts

● Use star tip, decorating bag, and remaining dark orange-tinted frosting to pipe individual stars atop orange section markings on both sides of cake; fill in sections with more stars. Apply sunflower nuts for seeds. Makes 6 servings.

Spider Web

2 cups creamy chocolate frosting *(use Chocolate Butter Frosting on page 88 or a creamy milk chocolate frosting mix for a 2-layer cake)*

2 8- *or* **9-inch round baked cake layers** *(use a recipe on pages 90-92 or a 2-layer-size cake mix)*

● Reserve about ½ cup of the creamy chocolate frosting for the top of the cake. Assemble the cake layers and frost only the sides with the remaining chocolate frosting.

Transform this eerie cake into an elegant dessert by leaving off the spider. The classic web pattern in the frosting is similar to the decorations used on European pastries and is impressive in its simple and delicate design.

½ cup sifted powdered sugar
¼ teaspoon vanilla
Milk

● For vanilla icing, stir together powdered sugar, vanilla, and enough milk (about 1½ tablespoons) to make icing of pouring consistency.

1 tablespoon corn syrup

● Stir corn syrup into reserved chocolate frosting; spread atop cake. Working quickly while frosting is soft, drizzle or pipe vanilla icing in 4 or 5 circles atop cake. Immediately draw 8 to 10 lines with a knife from the center of the cake to the edges at regular intervals.

Large red gumdrop
Red shoestring licorice, cut into 3-inch lengths

● For spider, place gumdrop on web design. Bend licorice pieces and place 4 on each side of the gumdrop, inserting ends into the cake. Makes 12 servings.

To create the web pattern in the frosting, drizzle the icing (or pipe with a writing tip in a parchment cone or pastry bag) in four or five circles around the top of the cake, starting 1 inch from the edge. Immediately draw a knife through the icing from the center of the cake to the edges at regular intervals.

A *Sunny-Side-Up Cake* makes a crazy birthday cake, April Fool's Day treat, or a "breakfast" in bed surprise for Mom on Mother's Day. Decorating this cake is so easy, even the kitchen-shy who can't fry an egg can do it.

Oven-going skillets are those with handles that can be removed or that can withstand oven temperatures (check the manufacturer's instructions). If you do not have an 8-inch oven-going skillet, bake the cake in an 8-inch round baking pan. Remove and cool the cake, then slip it into an ordinary 8-inch skillet and decorate.

Sunny-Side-Up Cake

Batter for a 1-layer-size cake *(use a recipe on pages 90-92 or a 1-layer-size cake mix)*

● For cake, grease an 8-inch oven-going skillet. Pour batter into skillet and bake in a 350° oven for 30 to 35 minutes or till a toothpick inserted in center comes out clean. Cool in skillet on a wire rack.

1 can sour cream white frosting *or* creamy white frosting
2 teaspoons ground cinnamon
2 apricot halves, well drained
2 round chocolate cookies *or* 2 chocolate covered peppermint patties (2½ inches in diameter)

● Reserve ½ cup of the frosting. Combine the remaining frosting and the cinnamon; spread atop cake to the edge of the skillet.
  Spread the reserved white frosting atop cake to form two "egg whites". Place apricot "yolks" in the center of "egg whites". Place cookies or mint patties alongside "eggs" to resemble sausage patties. Makes 6 servings.

Stitchery Sampler

1 8- *or* 9-inch round baked cake layer *(use a recipe on pages 90-92 or a 1-layer-size cake mix)*
2 cups creamy white frosting *(use Butter Frosting on page 88 or a creamy white frosting mix for a 2-layer cake)*

● Frost sides and top of cake with 1 cup of the frosting. With the edge of a ruler, mark lines across cake top in one direction about ⅛ inch apart. Repeat with perpendicular lines to resemble stitching canvas.

With a toothpick trace desired design on cake top. (Do this freehand or use a paper pattern.)

Paste food coloring (assorted colors)
Star tip *or* writing tip
Decorating bag *(see parchment cone on page 86 or use a pastry bag)*

● Divide ¾ cup of the remaining frosting into as many portions as the colors desired. Tint each portion with a different food coloring. With star tip and decorating bag, use tinted frosting to outline design with small stars resembling cross-stitches. Fill in outline with rows of stars. (Or, use writing tip to outline and fill in design with small diagonal dashes that resemble needlepoint stitches.)

1 yard of ¾-inch-wide ribbon
Ribbon tip

● Wrap ribbon around sides of cake, aligning with top edge; secure with tape. With ribbon tip and remaining untinted frosting, pipe a ruffle on sides of cake just below ribbon. Makes 12 servings.

A thimbleful of creativity is all it takes to sew up this cake. Just sketch a design on the cake with a toothpick, embroider with frosting stitches, and add a ribbon hoop and a frosting ruffle. Because you choose the design, a *Stitchery Sampler* fits any occasion.

To pipe a frosting ruffle, hold the ribbon tip with the wide end close to the surface of the cake and the narrow end away from the cake. Create the ruffle by touching the tip to the cake, then lifting off slightly, touching, then lifting off again as you move around the cake.

Cooperation Cake

1⅓ cups **Cream Cheese Frosting** *(see recipe, page 89)* **or 1 cup creamy white frosting** *(use Butter Frosting on page 88 or a creamy white frosting mix for a 1-layer cake)*
1 teaspoon **ground cinnamon**
1 **8-** *or* **9-inch round baked cake layer** *(use a recipe on pages 90-92 or a 1-layer-size cake mix)*
Assorted whole nuts such as almonds, cashews, peanuts, pecans, *or* **sunflower nuts**

● In a bowl stir together frosting and cinnamon; spread over the top of the cake layer.

Arrange the assorted nuts in a decorative pattern atop the frosted cake layer. (Suggestion: Place some of the nuts in a curved line across center of cake to resemble a stem. Arrange nuts in separate groups along the stem for blossoms. Then create a border around the top edge of the cake layer with one type of nut.)

Additional 8- or **9-inch round baked cake layers** *(see tip, far right)*
Chunk-style applesauce *or* **additional Cream Cheese Frosting** *or* **creamy white frosting**

● To assemble cake, spread ¾ cup chunk-style applesauce or ½ cup frosting between each cake layer. Top with the decorated cake layer.

A *Cooperation Cake* requires that each guest bring a round cake layer to be assembled at the serving site and topped with a layer you've decorated in advance.

This type of cake was traditional at pioneer weddings and was known as "stack cake". A bride's popularity could be measured by the number of wedding cake stacks she had and by the number of layers that were in each stack.

Since guests will probably bring different types of cake, your cake will have a rich variety of colors and flavors. Should you invite a crowd, limit the cakes in each stack to six and have several decorated cake tops ready.

Freezing Cakes

Cakes may be frozen unfrosted or frosted. To freeze unfrosted cakes, wrap the cooled layers in moisture-vaporproof material; seal, label, and freeze. Thaw the cakes in their wrapping at room temperature. Allow about 40 minutes for cupcakes, 1 hour for cake layers, and 3 hours for large cakes.

If cake is frosted, freeze it before wrapping. (Keep in mind that frosted cakes can become soggy and lose freshness when stored over a long period of time.) Thaw frosted or filled cakes, covered, in the refrigerator several hours or overnight.

Wedding Cake

Batter for two 2-layer-size cakes *(use a recipe on pages 90-92 or two 2-layer-size cake mixes)*

● Grease and lightly flour an 8x1½-inch round baking pan and a 10x2-inch round baking pan. Prepare the batter for one 2-layer-size cake. Divide the batter between the two pans, filling each about half full. Bake in a 350° oven for 25 to 30 minutes or till cakes test done. Cool in pans 10 minutes. Remove; cool completely on wire racks. Repeat with batter for second 2-layer-size cake.

Use one kind of cake batter for all the layers, or vary the flavors of the layers by using two different kinds of batters.

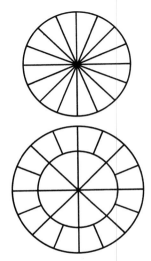

Pure White Creamy Frosting *(see recipe, page 89)*
Water *or* milk

● Level cakes, if tops are rounded.
　To assemble cake, spread one 10-inch layer with about ¾ cup of the frosting and top with second 10-inch layer. Continue layering by centering the two 8-inch layers atop the 10-inch layers and using about ½ cup frosting under each 8-inch layer.
　For undercoat, thin 1 cup of the frosting with a little water or milk; spread over assembled cake. Let dry about 2 hours or till firm.
　Reserve 1½ cups of the frosting for piping decoration. Frost the entire cake with the remaining frosting.

To cut the wedding cake for serving, remove the flowers. Remove the top tier to a plate; cut into 16 wedges and serve. For the bottom tier, cut a circle 2 inches in from the edge of the tier. Cut the entire tier into 8 wedges. Then cut each piece in the outer ring in half.

Star tip
Decorating bag *(see parchment cone on page 86 or use a pastry bag)*
Fresh *or* silk flowers

● Use star tip and decorating bag to pipe reserved frosting in garlands on sides of cake and in shell or star borders around top edges and bases of tiers. Arrange flowers atop cake and, if desired, around base. Makes 40 servings.

Dress Up the Sides of a Cake

Sometimes adding a simple decoration to the sides of a cake is just the touch you need to make an ordinary cake a spectacular one. What's more, you probably already have the items on hand for creating that special effect. Flaked, toasted, or tinted coconut adds texture and flavor to cakes and adheres well to frosting. A coating of chopped nuts on the sides serves the same purposes with a slightly more formal look. Candies of all shapes and colors also are suitable sidekicks on many cakes. And one of the simplest side-decorating techniques is to make impressions in the frosting with cookie cutters or the tines of a fork.

To make sugar mold eggs, combine the sugar and water in a bowl and knead with your fingers till the sugar is evenly moistened and feels like wet sand. Divide the mixture between three or four small bowls. Add a drop of a different liquid food coloring to each and knead till the mixture is evenly colored.

With your fingers, firmly pack some of the colored sugar mixture into an oval teaspoon (not a measuring spoon). Scrape off any excess sugar mixture from the top of the spoon.

Immediately unmold the colored sugar eggs by inverting the spoon over waxed paper and gently tapping out the molded sugar. Let the sugar mold eggs dry about 2 hours or till hardened.

Basket of Eggs

½ cup sugar
1 teaspoon water
  Liquid food coloring
    (assorted colors)

● In a bowl combine sugar and the 1 teaspoon water. Knead with your fingers till sugar is evenly moistened and feels like wet sand. Divide sugar mixture between three or four bowls. Add a drop of a different liquid food coloring to each and knead till evenly colored. Pack sugar firmly into a teaspoon (not a measuring spoon). Scrape excess sugar from top of spoon. Unmold at once by inverting spoon and tapping out sugar. Let dry about 2 hours.

Be sure to make the colored sugar eggs that decorate this cake before preparing the cake itself. The eggs take only a few minutes to shape, but need 2 hours to dry before applying to the cake.

3 cups creamy white
    frosting *(use Butter
    Frosting on page 88 or 2
    creamy white frosting mixes
    for a 2-layer cake)*
  Several drops liquid food
    coloring
2 8- *or* 9-inch round baked
    cake layers *(use a recipe
    on pages 90-92 or a 2-
    layer-size cake mix)*

● Reserve ½ cup of the creamy white frosting for the basket. Tint the remaining 2½ cups of frosting a pastel color with several drops of desired liquid food coloring. (If using frosting mix, refrigerate or freeze any unused frosting.) Assemble and frost the cake layers with the pastel-tinted frosting.

  Basket-weave tip *or* star
    tip
  Decorating bag *(see
    parchment cone on page
    86 or use a pastry bag)*

● Use reserved untinted frosting, basket-weave tip or star tip, and decorating bag to outline basket with handle on cake top. Arrange enough sugar mold eggs inside basket outline to fill basket (eggs may overlap). Pipe horizontal, then vertical lines of frosting over eggs for weave of basket. Make the lines about 1½ inches apart so eggs can be seen.

  Few drops water
1 *or* 2 drops green liquid
    food coloring
¼ cup flaked coconut
  About 1 cup gumdrops

● In a small screw-top jar combine the few drops water and green liquid food coloring. Add coconut; secure lid. Shake till all of the coconut is tinted. Sprinkle the tinted coconut atop cake around basket. If desired, pat additional tinted coconut onto sides of cake. Arrange gumdrops around bottom of cake. Makes 12 servings.

Lady's Hat

Batter for a 2-layer-size cake *(use a recipe on pages 90-92 or a 2-layer-size cake mix)*

● Grease and flour a 9x1½-inch round baking pan and a 7-inch pie plate. Pour 3¼ cups of the batter into the 9x1½-inch pan and 1¼ cups batter into the 7-inch pie plate. Bake in a 350° oven till cakes test done, about 25 minutes for 7-inch pie plate and about 30 minutes for 9x1½-inch pan. (Bake any remaining batter as cupcakes in muffin pans lined with paper bake cups in the 350° oven about 20 minutes.) Cool 10 minutes in pans. Remove; cool completely.

2 cups creamy white frosting *(use Butter Frosting on page 88 or a creamy white frosting mix for a 2-layer cake)*
Pink *or* red paste food coloring

● Reserve ¼ cup of the frosting for hat ribbon. Tint remaining frosting pale pink with food coloring. Spread about ¼ cup of the pink-tinted frosting on the top (widest side) of the pie plate cake. Place off-center, frosting side down, atop the 9-inch cake layer so cake edges meet on one side. Frost entire cake with remaining pink-tinted frosting, building up top to make a rounded crown.

Leaf tip
Decorating bag *(see parchment cone on page 86 or use a pastry bag)*
Small gumdrops

● Using leaf tip and decorating bag, pipe the reserved untinted frosting in a continuous ribbon around crown of hat. Use gumdrops to make Gumdrop Roses (see instructions below). Make leaves by rolling out gumdrops and cutting leaf shapes with a knife. Place two or three roses on front of hat; arrange leaves around roses. Makes 12 servings.

***Gumdrop Roses:* Place gumdrops on a clean surface sprinkled with sugar. Sprinkle again with sugar. With a rolling pin roll gumdrops into ovals. Cut ovals in half crosswise. Starting at one corner, roll up a half-oval diagonally to form rose center. Press on additional half-ovals, shaping the outer edges to resemble petals. Trim base if necessary.**

Gentleman's Hat

2 8-inch round baked cake layers *(use a recipe on pages 90-92 or a 2-layer-size cake mix)*	● Level cake tops if too rounded. Place one cake layer, top side up, on the cardboard round. Spread with about ¼ cup of the frosting. Top with remaining cake layer, top side down. Stir the cinnamon into remaining frosting; spread on sides and top of cake and on exposed surface of cardboard. Draw the tines of a fork through the frosting to give it a rough texture.
1 10-inch cardboard round	
2 cups creamy white frosting *(use Butter Frosting on page 88 or a creamy white frosting mix for a 2-layer cake)*	
2 teaspoons ground cinnamon	
22 milk chocolate stars	● Press milk chocolate stars around base of cake for hat band. Serves 12.

Sheriff's Badge

2 cups creamy chocolate frosting *(use Chocolate Butter Frosting on page 88 or a creamy chocolate fudge frosting mix for a 2-layer cake)*

2 8- *or* **9-inch round baked cake layers** *(use a recipe on pages 90-92 or a 2-layer-size cake mix)*

● Reserve 2 tablespoons of the creamy chocolate frosting for piping the outline of the sheriff's badge onto the cake.

Use all of the remaining creamy chocolate frosting to assemble and frost the cake layers.

To make the star pattern, use a compass to draw a circle with a 2½-inch radius on a piece of paper. Without adjusting the compass, place the point of the compass at any point of the circle outline. Make a mark where the compass crosses the circle to the right of the point. Move the point of the compass to the mark on the right, swing the pencil to the right, and make another mark on the circle. Continue around the circle till you've made six marks.

Drawing compass

● To make pattern, on a piece of paper draw a circle that has a 2½-inch radius. Without adjusting compass, place the compass point at any point of the circle outline. Make a mark where compass crosses circle to right of point. Move the compass point to the mark on the right and swing pencil to the right to make another mark where compass crosses circle. Continue marks around circle. With a pencil and ruler, connect marks as shown below in double triangle design to form star. Cut out pattern.

1 tube yellow decorator icing and plastic writing tip

● Place paper star atop frosted cake. Trace around star with a toothpick. Remove pattern. Retrace lines and fill in design with yellow decorator icing and writing tip. With a knife or metal spatula, smooth decorator icing.

1 teaspoon unsweetened cocoa powder
Parchment cone *(see instructions, page 86)*
Semisweet chocolate pieces

● Stir cocoa powder into the reserved chocolate frosting. Snip a tiny hole in the tip of parchment cone and pipe reserved frosting atop star to outline badge and write message. Place a chocolate piece at each point of star and around top and bottom edges of cake. Serves 12.

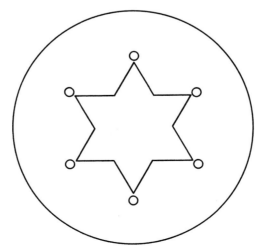

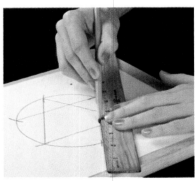

With a pencil and a ruler, connect the marks in a double triangle design to form a star as shown. Cut out the star pattern and place in the center of the cake top as shown in the diagram at left.

Butterfly Cutout

1 8- *or* 9-inch round baked cake layer *(use a recipe on pages 90-92 or a 1-layer-size cake mix)*

● Follow directions at right for inserting toothpicks in cake, scoring curved lines with the tip of a knife, and cutting through the cake. Let cut pieces of cake stand 1 to 2 hours or till the cut edges are slightly dry.

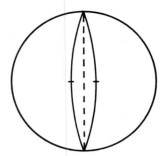

2 cups creamy white frosting *(use Butter Frosting on page 88 or a creamy white frosting mix for a 2-layer cake)*
Yellow paste food coloring
Orange paste food coloring
1 teaspoon unsweetened cocoa powder

● Divide and tint the frosting as follows: tint 1¼ cups with yellow food coloring, tint ½ cup with orange food coloring, and tint ¼ cup with cocoa powder.
    Frost the sides and tops of the two larger pieces with the yellow-tinted frosting. Frost the center piece with half of the orange-tinted frosting. Place wing pieces, cut side out, on either side of the center piece so pieces touch.

Stick two toothpicks on opposite edges of the cake for cutting guides. Position the cake so an imaginary line between the toothpicks is straight up and down in front of you. Measure between the toothpicks to find the center; insert toothpicks ½ inch to the left and right of center. With the tip of a sharp knife, score two curved lines in the cake as shown above, connecting the toothpicks on the edges with those near the center. Cut completely through the cake at the score marks.

Star tip
Decorating bag *(see parchment cone on page 86 or use a pastry bag)*

● Working 1 inch from edge, use star tip, decorating bag, and remaining orange-tinted frosting to pipe a series of stars in a design on wing pieces, as shown in diagram below. If desired, pipe additional stars around the design.

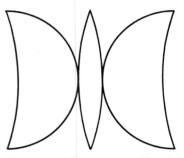

Writing tip
Black shoestring licorice (optional)

● Use writing tip to pipe chocolate frosting inside the orange design on the wings and along the edge of the center piece. If desired, cut shoestring licorice into 3-inch lengths and insert in cake for feelers. Makes 6 servings.

Frost and arrange the two "wings" next to the "body" of the butterfly so the cut sides of the larger pieces face out.

Decorate the assembled butterfly by piping on frosting. Add a finishing touch to the cake with feelers made of shoestring licorice.

Gingerbread Village

2 14½-ounce packages gingerbread mix	● Prepare each gingerbread mix separately according to package directions, except mix in a bowl with a fork and bake each in a greased and floured 9x1½-inch round baking pan. Cool in pans 10 minutes. Remove; cool completely. Leave one layer uncut; level top if necessary. Cut the other layer as shown in diagram, below left.	To make a mailbox for your *Gingerbread Village*, cut out a 1x½-inch piece of paper. Make a crease ¼ inch from one of the short ends. Arch the remaining length of the paper over so the two ends meet. Tape ends together. Poke a toothpick through the flat side of the mailbox and insert in the cake.
2 cups sifted powdered sugar **¼ cup water**	● For glaze, stir together powdered sugar and water. Use a pastry brush to brush glaze over all surfaces of cake pieces. Let dry on a wire rack.	
2 cups fluffy white frosting *(use Fluffy White Frosting on page 88 or a fluffy white frosting mix for a 2-layer cake)* **Pearl sugar *or* crushed sugar cubes**	● Frost top of uncut layer. Place platform piece (A) atop uncut layer, as shown in diagram, below right; frost platform. Arrange remaining pieces as shown, with the flat bases down. Frost tops of pieces and sides of base, swirling frosting to resemble snowdrifts. Sprinkle with pearl sugar or crushed sugar cubes. Cut chimneys from cake scraps; insert in frosting atop houses. If desired, add mailbox (see directions, right). Serves 16.	

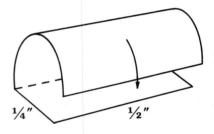

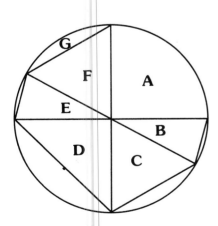

Cut one layer, as shown above, for the village houses, platform, and bridge. Cut flat bases on all houses (B through F). Cut chimneys from the cake scraps.

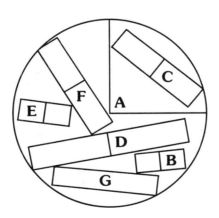

Arrange the cut pieces atop the uncut layer as shown above. Add chimneys to some of the housetops after frosting.

Elegant Gâteau

⅓ **cup sliced almonds**
2 **cups creamy white frosting** (*use Butter Frosting on page 88 or a creamy white frosting mix for a 2-layer cake*)
1 **8- or 9-inch round baked cake layer** (*use a recipe on pages 90-92 or a 1-layer-size cake mix*)
6 **maraschino cherries, halved and drained well on paper toweling**

● If desired, toast the almonds by spreading them in a single layer on a baking sheet. Place in a 350° oven about 10 minutes or till light brown, stirring nuts often. Cool completely.

Reserve ½ cup of the frosting. Frost sides and top of the cake layer with remaining frosting. Gently press the almonds onto the cake sides. With a toothpick, make 12 marks an equal distance apart around the cake top (in the positions of numbers on a clock face). Top each mark with a cherry half.

Star tip
Decorating bag (*see parchment cone on page 86 or use a pastry bag*)

● Using star tip and decorating bag, pipe reserved frosting in scallops around the cherries. Pipe a star at the point of each scallop. Makes 6 servings.

The cakes on these two pages look like cakes you would see in a Viennese pastry shop window. Because the secret to elegant-looking desserts like these is their simplicity, you'll be surprised at how easily you can duplicate them in your kitchen.

Viennese-Style Mocha Torte

6 **tablespoons butter** *or* **margarine**
4 **to 5 cups sifted powdered sugar**
1½ **teaspoons instant coffee crystals**
¼ **cup milk**
1 **square (1 ounce) unsweetened chocolate, melted and cooled**

● In small mixer bowl beat butter or margarine till light and fluffy. Gradually beat in about 2 cups of the powdered sugar. Divide mixture in half.

Dissolve coffee crystals in 2 tablespoons of the milk; beat into one half of butter mixture. Beat cooled, melted chocolate and the remaining 2 tablespoons milk into the other half of the butter mixture.

Beat enough powdered sugar (about 1 cup) into each half to make frosting of spreading consistency.

1 **8- or 9-inch round baked cake layer** (*use a recipe on pages 90-92 or a 1-layer-size cake mix*)
⅓ **cup chopped nuts** *or* **almond brickle pieces**

● Reserve half of the coffee frosting; spread remaining on cake sides. Press nuts or brickle pieces into frosting on cake sides. Spread chocolate frosting on cake top. With a toothpick, make 13 marks an equal distance apart around edge of cake top and in center.

Star tip
Decorating bag (*see parchment cone on page 86 or use a pastry bag*)
13 **milk chocolate stars**

● Using star tip and decorating bag, pipe reserved coffee frosting in designs starting with circles around the 13 marks and drawing tails to center of cake. Pipe a swirl of frosting in the center. Place a chocolate star in the center of each circle. Makes 6 servings.

To cover the sides of the cake with chopped nuts or brickle pieces, place the cake on a piece of waxed paper and balance it in one hand. Hold the nuts in the other hand. Tilt the cake toward the nuts and gently press the nuts onto the frosting. Turn the cake on your hand and continue applying the nuts till the sides of the cake are well covered.

Old MacDonald's Farm

1½ **recipes Hot Milk Sponge Cake Batter** *(see recipe, page 93)*

● Pour 2½ cups of the batter into a greased and floured 8x8x2-inch baking pan. Pour remaining 2 cups into a greased and floured 8x4x2-inch loaf pan. Bake in a 350° oven till done: about 20 minutes for square pan and about 25 minutes for loaf pan. Cool 10 minutes in pans. Remove; cool on wire racks.

½ **cup shredded coconut**
  Few drops water
  Few drops yellow liquid food coloring
8 **to 10 round sandwich cookies**
3 **cups creamy white frosting** *(use Butter Frosting on page 88 or 2 creamy white frosting mixes for a 2-layer cake)*

● Meanwhile, stir together coconut, water, and yellow food coloring. Spread on waxed paper to dry.
   For silo, secure sandwich cookies one atop another using a small amount of frosting between each. Let dry till firm.
   If necessary, slice off tops of cooled cakes to level before assembling barn.

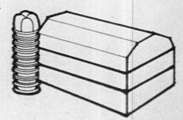

  Red paste food coloring
4 **teaspoons unsweetened cocoa powder**
  Sliced blanched almonds *or* **bite-size shredded rice** *or* **corn squares**

● Divide and tint remaining frosting as follows: tint 1½ cups with red paste food coloring, ¾ cup with cocoa powder, and leave ½ cup untinted. (If using frosting mix, refrigerate or freeze unused frosting.) Reserve 2 tablespoons untinted frosting for piping. Cut square cake in half crosswise to form two rectangles. To assemble barn, spread about half of the remaining untinted frosting atop one rectangle. Top with other rectangle; spread with untinted frosting. Top with loaf cake, top side down.
   To shape roof, slice off the long edges of loaf cake at an angle, as shown in diagram, right. Frost silo and barn sides with the red-tinted frosting, using up-and-down strokes to resemble barn siding. Frost roof with the chocolate frosting. Layer almonds or attach rows of cereal squares on roof for shingles.

  Writing tip
  Decorating bag *(see parchment cone on page 86 or use a pastry bag)*
1 **chocolate-covered marshmallow-filled cookie**

● Use writing tip and decorating bag to pipe reserved plain frosting on barn for door and hayloft. Place cookie silo next to barn. Arrange tinted coconut around base of barn and gently press some onto frosting near hayloft. Secure chocolate marshmallow-filled cookie to top of silo with any remaining frosting. Serves 14.

Shiny Apples

3 to 6 small fresh leaves
¼ cup semisweet chocolate pieces

● Wash leaves and dry thoroughly. In a small, heavy saucepan melt chocolate pieces over low heat, stirring constantly. With a clean, small paintbrush, brush the melted chocolate on the undersides of the leaves, building up layers of chocolate to make sturdy leaves (see photo, right). Wipe off any melted chocolate that may have run onto the front of the leaves. Place on waxed paper-lined baking sheet and refrigerate or freeze till hardened.

To make chocolate leaves, use a clean small paint-brush to brush melted chocolate pieces on the underside of small fresh leaves, building up layers of chocolate to make sturdy leaves.

Batter for a 1-layer-size cake *(use a recipe on pages 90-92 or a 1-layer-size cake mix)*

● Meanwhile, grease and flour a 6-unit (1 cup size) fluted tube pan. Divide batter among the units. Bake in a 350° oven about 25 minutes or till cakes test done. Cool in pan 5 minutes. Remove from pan; cool on a wire rack.

2½ cups fluffy white frosting *(use Fluffy White Frosting on page 88 or a fluffy white frosting mix for a 2-layer cake)*
Red, yellow, *and/or* green paste food coloring

● Prepare frosting, adding red, yellow, or green food coloring as you beat. (Or, prepare frosting, divide into thirds, and tint each portion a different color.) For each apple, spread the flat side of one cake with a small amount of frosting, spreading almost to edges. Top with another cake, flat side down. Generously frost with the remaining frosting. Make frosting thicker where cakes are joined to give apples a rounded shape.

When peeling the real leaves away from the chocolate leaves, avoid touching the chocolate as much as possible to keep it from melting.

Stick cinnamon

● Insert a piece of stick cinnamon in the center of each apple for stem. Just before serving, peel real leaf away from chocolate leaf, touching the chocolate as little as possible (see photo, right). Gently press one or two chocolate leaves atop each apple next to cinnamon stem. Makes 3 cakes (6 servings).

The Great Pumpkin

Batter for two 2-layer-size cakes (use recipes on pages 90-92 or two 2-layer-size cake mixes)	● Divide batter between two greased and floured 10-inch fluted tube pans. Bake in a 350° oven about 45 minutes or till cakes test done. Cool in pans 10 minutes. Remove; cool on wire racks.
5 cups fluffy white frosting (use Fluffy White Frosting on page 88 or 2 fluffy white frosting mixes for a 2-layer cake) **Orange paste food coloring**	● Reserve ½ cup of the frosting for stem; cover. Tint remaining frosting with orange food coloring. Spread the flat side of one cake with about ½ cup of the tinted frosting, spreading almost to edges. Top with remaining cake, flat side down. Frost entire cake, making frosting thicker where cakes are joined to give pumpkin a rounded shape. Use a metal spatula or table knife to make grooves in frosting to resemble lines on a pumpkin.
Green paste food coloring **1 flat-bottomed ice cream cone**	● Tint the reserved frosting with green food coloring; frost the outside and bottom of the ice cream cone and insert the cone, bottom up, in center of cake for stem. Makes 24 servings.

To make a "carved" pumpkin, assemble (but don't frost) the cake and mark eyes and mouth on the side of the cake by making shallow cuts with a knife or by outlining with toothpicks. Frost up to the marks or toothpicks, leaving the area for the eyes and mouth unfrosted. Remove toothpicks if used.

Lollipops

1½ recipes **Hot Milk Sponge Cake Batter** *(see recipe, page 93)*	● Grease and flour a 15x10x1-inch baking pan. Pour batter into prepared pan. Bake in a 350° oven for 20 to 25 minutes or till done. Cool in pan 10 minutes. Remove; cool completely.	Decorate these *Lollipops* with sweets such as candy-coated milk chocolate pieces, red cinnamon candies, or candy corn. Or cut and piece different flavors of rolled fruit leather for a unique and colorful decoration.
2 cups **creamy white frosting** *(use Butter Frosting on page 88 or a creamy white frosting mix for a 2-layer cake)* **Assorted candies** *and/or* **rolled fruit leather** **Wooden sticks**	● Press the open end of a clean 4- or 4½-inch-wide can into cake to cut six or seven circles. Frost sides and one flat surface of each circle with frosting. Gently press candies or fruit leather on top surface and onto the sides. Insert a wooden stick into the side of or underneath each cake. Serves 6 or 7.	

Jelly Jars

6 straight-sided half-pint **jelly jars with metal rings** 2 cups **all-purpose flour** 1 teaspoon **baking soda** ½ teaspoon **salt**	● Grease the jelly jars. In a mixing bowl stir together the all-purpose flour, the baking soda, and the salt.	Preserve a friendship or start a new one with some homemade *Jelly Jars*. Steam the cakes right in the jars over boiling water in a kettle. Top the cakes with frosting lids, metal jelly jar rings, and some hand-picked words for a personal touch.
¾ cup **sugar** ½ cup **butter** *or* **margarine** 2 **eggs** 1 teaspoon **vanilla**	● In large mixer bowl beat sugar, butter or margarine, eggs, and vanilla with electric mixer on medium speed till the mixture is light and fluffy.	
1 cup **buttermilk** 1 cup **chopped pecans** 1 10-ounce jar **maraschino cherries, drained and chopped (1 cup)**	● Add flour mixture and buttermilk alternately to butter mixture, beating just till blended after each addition. Fold in nuts and cherries. Pour about ⅔ cup batter into each jar; cover with foil. Place jars on rack in large kettle with 1 inch simmering water. Cover and steam about 30 minutes or till a toothpick inserted in center comes out clean. Cool in jars 10 minutes. Remove from jars; cool completely. Wash jars; replace cakes.	
1 cup **creamy white frosting** *(use Butter Frosting on page 88 or a creamy white frosting mix for a 1-layer cake)* **Paste food coloring** **Writing tip** **Decorating bag** *(see parchment cone on page 86 or use a pastry bag)*	● Reserve ¼ cup of the frosting. Spread 1 to 2 tablespoons of the remaining frosting atop each cooled cake in jar. Make crisscross lines in the frosting with fork tines to resemble stitching canvas. Secure the metal rings to jars. Tint the reserved frosting with desired food coloring. Use writing tip, decorating bag, and the tinted frosting to pipe words atop jars. Makes 6 cakes (12 servings).	

Evening News

Batter for Jelly Roll Cake *(see recipe, page 94)* **Sifted powdered sugar** ½ **cup jelly** *or* **jam**	● Bake batter for Jelly Roll Cake according to recipe directions and turn out onto towel sprinkled with sifted powdered sugar. Instead of rolling from narrow end, start from wide end and roll warm cake with towel; cool on wire rack. Unroll; spread with jelly or jam to within 1 inch of edges. Roll up cake.
2 **cups creamy white frosting** *(use Butter Frosting on page 88 or a creamy white frosting mix for a 2-layer cake)* **Black paste food coloring** **Newspaper photograph (optional)** **Writing tip** **Decorating bag** *(see parchment cone on page 86 or use a pastry bag)*	● Tint ½ cup of the frosting with black food coloring. Frost curved surface of cake with the remaining untinted frosting, leaving ends unfrosted. Gently press the edge of a ruler into frosting lengthwise across cake to mark area for newspaper headline and columns. If photograph is desired, cut a piece of waxed paper to fit newspaper photo. Tape waxed paper to back of the photo; attach to cake with a little frosting. Using writing tip and decorating bag, pipe black-tinted frosting across cake for newspaper headlines and column print. Makes 10 servings.

Graduation Diploma: **Prepare** *Evening News* **as directed at left,** *except* **tint half of the reserved ½ cup frosting with** *red paste food coloring* **and half with** *black paste food coloring.* **With** *writing tip,* **pipe black-tinted frosting across cake to spell desired message. With** *ribbon or leaf tip,* **pipe red-tinted frosting around center of cake to form ribbon and bow.**

Cappuccino Coffee Cup Cakes

½ **cup butter** *or* **margarine** ¼ **cup water** 2 **tablespoons unsweetened cocoa powder** 1 **tablespoon instant coffee crystals**	● Grease four 8-ounce oven-going coffee cups or mugs. In a saucepan combine butter, water, cocoa powder, and coffee crystals. Bring to boiling, stirring constantly. Remove from heat.
1 **cup all-purpose flour** 1 **cup sugar** ½ **teaspoon baking soda** ¼ **teaspoon salt** 1 **slightly beaten egg** ¼ **cup buttermilk** 1 **teaspoon vanilla**	● In a mixing bowl stir together flour, sugar, baking soda, and salt; stir in egg, buttermilk, and vanilla. Stir in cocoa mixture. Fill the greased coffee cups about ½ full with batter. Place cups in a shallow baking pan. Bake in a 350° oven for 25 to 30 minutes or till a toothpick inserted near center comes out clean.
Whipped cream **Ground cinnamon** *or* **nutmeg**	● Just before serving, dollop each with whipped cream and sprinkle with cinnamon or nutmeg. Serve warm or cool. Makes 4 servings.

Decorate Cakes with Gumdrops

You'll be surprised at how easy, yet impressive, cake decorating can be with gumdrops. Once flattened, they can be cut into shapes, like the holly leaves on this page, or rolled up to form roses, similar to the ones on page 48. To flatten gumdrops, sprinkle sugar on a cutting board or counter top to prevent sticking. Place one gumdrop at a time on the sugared surface, sprinkle with more sugar, and roll out the gumdrop with a rolling pin. Then cut or shape as desired.

Little Yule Logs

Batter for Chocolate Jelly Roll Cake *(see recipe, page 94)*
½ **cup apricot preserves**

● Bake and turn out cake according to recipe directions. Instead of rolling from narrow end, start from wide end and roll cake and towel; cool. Unroll; spread with apricot preserves. Roll up cake.

For a shortcut, frost these logs with canned frosting. You'll need about ½ can of white frosting and 1 can of chocolate frosting.

1 **cup creamy white frosting** *(use Butter Frosting on page 88 or a creamy white frosting mix for a 1-layer cake)*
2 **cups creamy chocolate frosting** *(use Chocolate Butter Frosting on page 88 or a creamy milk chocolate frosting mix for a 2-layer cake)*

● Slice roll crosswise into four equal logs. Frost ends of logs with white frosting. Spread remaining portion of logs with chocolate frosting, streaking frosting from end to end with metal spatula or a fork to resemble bark.

Sugar
Small green gumdrops
Red cinnamon candies

● For holly leaves, sprinkle sugar on a cutting board. Place one gumdrop at a time on sugared board; sprinkle with more sugar. With a rolling pin, flatten each gumdrop into an oval. Follow the instructions below for cutting out holly leaves. Press gently into frosting atop log along with cinnamon candies for holly berries. Makes 4 cakes (8 to 10 servings).

To cut holly leaves from rolled-out gumdrops, firmly press the tip of a spoon around the outside of the gumdrops, cutting away tiny pieces to make scalloped edges.

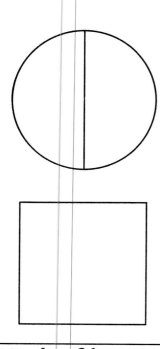

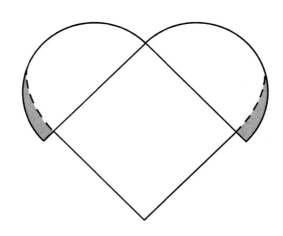

This is the perfect cake for a bridal shower, wedding anniversary, or Valentine's Day. Best of all, you don't need a special heart-shape pan to make it. Just cut a 9-inch round cake in half crosswise and attach the halves to two adjacent sides of an 8-inch square cake.

Heart Cake

Batter for a 2-layer-size cake *(use a recipe on pages 90-92 or a 2-layer-size cake mix)*

2 cups creamy white frosting *(use Butter Frosting on page 88 or a creamy white frosting mix for a 2-layer cake)*

● Pour half of the batter into a greased and floured 9-inch round baking pan. Pour the other half into a greased and floured 8x8x2-inch baking pan. Bake in a 350° oven about 30 minutes or till cakes test done. Let cool in pans 10 minutes. Remove; cool completely.

If layers are uneven, level the taller layer so it's the same height as the shorter layer. Cut the round layer in half crosswise; spread frosting on the cut edges. Attach frosted sides of round halves to two adjacent sides of the square cake. Trim extending edges of round halves if necessary.

Pink *or* red paste food coloring

● Reserve ½ cup of the frosting for piping design on cake. Tint remaining frosting pastel pink with pink or red food coloring. Frost sides and top of cake with pink-tinted frosting.

Writing tip
Decorating bag *(see parchment cone on page 86 or use a pastry bag)*
Star tip

● Use writing tip, decorating bag, and reserved untinted frosting to pipe a frilly design around the outer 2 inches of the cake top. Write a message in the center of the cake. With the star tip, pipe a border of individual stars around the top edge of the cake. Makes 12 servings.

Instead of piping a design on the cake, try one of these simple decorations:

Apply tinted coconut or small candies.

Swirl the frosting in small circles or heart shapes.

Make scallops in the frosting with the tip of a spoon.

Combine the ideas, using one on the cake top and another on the sides.

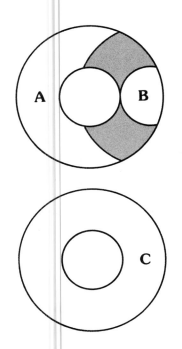

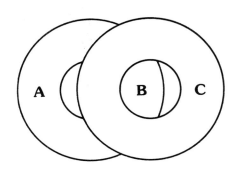

Linked Sweetheart Rings

Here's how to cut and link the rings. Cut a section from one ring (about ⅓ of the ring) so the remainder of the ring (A) will fit up against the uncut ring (C). From the cutout piece, cut a smaller piece (B) to fit inside the uncut ring and continue the circle. Attach the pieces with some of the untinted frosting before completely frosting the outside.

Batter for a 2-layer-size cake *(use a recipe on pages 90-92 or a 2-layer-size cake mix)*	● Grease and flour two 5-cup oven-proof ring molds. Divide batter between prepared pans. Bake in a 350° oven about 25 minutes or till cakes test done. Cool in pans 10 minutes. Remove cakes; cool completely.
2 cups creamy white frosting *(use Butter Frosting on page 88 or a creamy white frosting mix for a 2-layer cake)* **Yellow paste food coloring**	● Tint ¼ cup of the creamy white frosting desired shade with yellow paste food coloring. Leave the remaining frosting untinted.
	● From one cake, cut off ⅓ of the ring as shown above. From the cutout piece, cut a smaller piece (B) to fit inside the uncut ring (C) and continue the circle with (A). Spread some untinted frosting on the cut sides of the cake pieces and attach as shown to form linked rings. Frost entire cake with the remaining untinted frosting.
Writing tip **Decorating bag** *(see parchment cone on page 86 or use a pastry bag)* **Star tip**	● Use writing tip, decorating bag, and yellow-tinted frosting to pipe names on the lower part of the rings. For border, use star tip to pipe individual stars around base of cake. Makes 12 servings.

To make frosting a golden yellow color, add a tiny amount of red paste food coloring to the yellow-tinted frosting. You'll need only a touch of red; any more will turn the frosting orange.

Moon Rocket
(see recipe, page 72)

Victory Basketball
(see recipe, page 71)

Candy-Car Racetrack
(see recipe, page 73)

Baseball Caps
(see recipe, page 70)

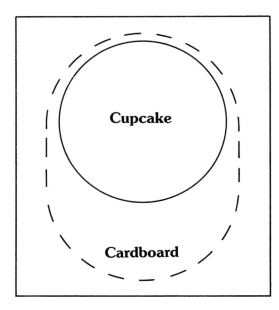

Cupcake

Cardboard

Little leaguers at your house can help cut the cardboard bills for these cap cakes. Place a cupcake, top side down, on a piece of thin cardboard. (If the cupcake is too peaked, slice off the top of the cupcake.) Use a pencil to trace around the cupcake. Then draw an oblong bill extending from the cupcake on one side. Cut out with a scissors; then use as a pattern to make the remaining bills.

Baseball Caps

Pictured on page 69—

12 baked cupcakes *(use recipe for Yellow Cupcakes on page 90 or a 1-layer-size cake mix)*
Thin cardboard

● If tops of cupcakes are peaked, slice off tops so inverted cupcakes will rest on cardboard bases.
　To make bases of caps, place one cupcake, upside down, on a piece of cardboard. Use a pencil to trace around the outer edge of the cupcake. Then draw an oblong bill extending from cupcake on one side (see diagram above). Cut out with scissors. Use this shape as a pattern to trace and cut out 11 more cardboard bases. Cover each base with foil.

When it's your turn to bring treats, treat them to *Baseball Caps* instead of ordinary cupcakes. Turn the caps into scout caps, farmer hats, army hats, or construction hardhats by varying the frosting color and decoration. Use an actual hat or a picture of one as a model to make the cakes as true-to-life as possible.

4 cups creamy white frosting *(use Butter Frosting on page 88 or 2 creamy white frosting mixes for a 2-layer cake)*
Paste food coloring (assorted colors)

● Reserve ½ cup of the frosting for piping. Tint with food coloring or leave untinted. Tint remaining frosting with desired food coloring.
　For each cap, dab a small amount of frosting in center of cardboard base. Place a cupcake, upside down, atop frosting. Spread frosting over cupcake and bill, shaping frosting with a metal spatula to resemble baseball cap.

Writing tip
Decorating bag *(see parchment cone on page 86 or use a pastry bag)*

● Use writing tip, decorating bag, and reserved frosting to pipe name on front of cap above bill and to add a dot for button atop cap. Makes 12 servings.

Victory Basketball

Pictured on page 68—

1 recipe Hot Milk Sponge Cake Batter *(see recipe, page 93)*	● Grease and flour two oven-proof 1-quart glass mixing bowls. Divide batter between prepared bowls. Bake in a 350° oven about 20 minutes or till cakes test done. Cool in the bowls 10 minutes. Remove; cool completely. Level flat side of cakes.	**Originally, basketballs were made by piecing together and sewing flaps of leather around a sphere to make a smooth ball. Though other materials have replaced the leather pieces, the sewing lines have remained. Use a real basketball for a model to duplicate these lines on your cake.**
2 cups creamy white frosting *(use Butter Frosting on page 88 or a creamy white frosting mix for a 2-layer cake)* **Orange paste food coloring** **Textured towel**	● Reserve ¼ cup of the frosting for piping. Tint remaining frosting with orange food coloring. Spread the leveled side of one cake with some of the orange-tinted frosting; top with other cake, leveled side down. Frost outside of entire cake with remaining orange-tinted frosting. Allow to dry slightly. Place a textured towel over cake; press gently to give frosting a rough appearance.	
Black paste food coloring **Writing tip** **Decorating bag** *(see parchment cone on page 86 or use a pastry bag)*	● Use a toothpick to mark basketball lines and, if desired, lettering. Tint reserved frosting with black food coloring. Use writing tip and decorating bag to pipe lines and lettering on cake with the black-tinted frosting. Makes 8 to 10 servings.	

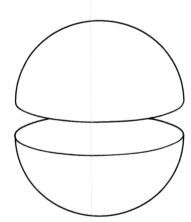

Texturing Frosting

Some cakes look better when the frosting is slightly bumpy. The *Victory Basketball* above is a good example, and the *Football Field* on pages 6 and 7 also could be roughed up. To give the surface this rough texture, you'll need a clean towel with a nubby pile, such as a terry-cloth hand towel. First frost the cake smooth and let it dry about 30 minutes or till the frosting loses its sticky quality. Then lay the towel over the cake and press gently to imprint the texture into the frosting.

Moon Rocket

Pictured on page 68—

1 **Jelly Roll Cake** *or* **Chocolate Jelly Roll Cake** *(see recipes, page 94)* *or* **purchased jelly roll cake**
2 **cups creamy white frosting** *(use Butter Frosting on page 88 or a creamy white frosting mix for a 2-layer cake)*
1 **tube blue decorator icing and plastic writing tip**

● With a knife, trim one end of the jelly roll cake to form a point. Frost entire jelly roll cake with the creamy white frosting. With a toothpick, trace lines and rivets in frosting (see photo on page 68). Retrace using blue decorator icing and plastic writing tip.

Kids will get a lift out of seeing themselves in the window of a *Moon Rocket* cake. To do this, cover the front and back of a small-scale school picture with clear plastic wrap to protect it. Then attach it to the cake with some frosting and pipe decorator icing around it to make a window.

Thin cardboard
3 **pointed ice cream cones**

● Cut three right triangles from the cardboard; cover with foil. Insert in sides and top of cake for rocket fins. With a sharp knife, use a gentle sawing motion to cut ice cream cones 1½ inches from pointed ends. Insert tips in rocket bottom for exhaust pipes. Serves 8 to 10.

Makeshift Cake Plates

The platter you use to serve a cake on can make or break your work of art. For best support, surfaces should be flat and slightly larger than the cake. One way to be sure your platter will work is to make your own. Stiff cardboard is an easy and inexpensive surface to use. Cut the cardboard to fit your cake. Then cover it with foil or decorative paper that has a protective finish. (We made the "crater plate" for the Moon Rocket on page 68 by forming rings out of foil and taping them to the cardboard before covering the entire surface with foil.) Festive baskets, boxes, or trays lined with foil or plastic wrap also make clever cake plates. Just be sure they don't compete with the design of the cake itself.

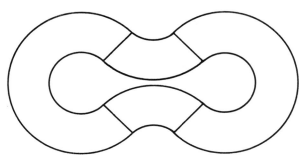

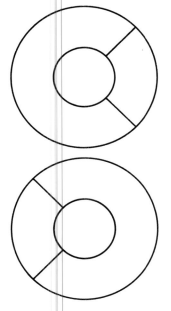

To assemble the racetrack, first cut off about ¼ from each ring-shape cake. Turn each piece so the inner sides face out. Spread frosting between the cut pieces and assemble them into the track. Then frost the entire cake.

Candy-Car Racetrack

Pictured on page 69—

Make paper flags and attach them to the *Candy-Car Racetrack* with toothpicks. Each color of flag has a meaning.

Green: Start the race.
Yellow: Caution.
Black: Racer is disqualified.
Red: Stop the race completely.
White: One lap to go.
Black-and-white checkered: Finish line.

Batter for a 2-layer-size cake *(use a recipe on pages 90-92 or a 2-layer-size cake mix)*

● Grease and flour two 5-cup ovenproof ring molds. Divide batter between prepared pans. Bake in a 350° oven about 25 minutes or till cakes test done. Cool in pans 10 minutes. Remove; cool completely.

Level rounded cake tops. Cut off about ¼ from each ring as shown in diagram, above left. Rearrange pieces as shown, above right.

---

3 cups creamy chocolate frosting *(use Chocolate Butter Frosting on page 88 or 2 creamy milk chocolate frosting mixes for a 2-layer cake)*

● Attach cut pieces of cake with some of the creamy chocolate frosting. Use remaining to frost sides and top of cake. (If using frosting mix, refrigerate or freeze any unused frosting.)

---

1 tube white decorator icing and plastic writing tip
Small round candies (any variety)
Wrapped hard oval candies

● With decorator icing and writing tip, make dotted lines around center of top surface of cake for lane markings in the form of a figure eight.

To make race cars, pipe dots of decorator icing onto small round candies and attach to sides of hard oval candies for wheels. Place candy cars in lanes on cake. If desired, construct and attach racing flags to cake. Makes 12 servings.

Easter Chick

1 recipe Hot Milk Sponge Cake Batter *(see recipe, page 93)*

● Grease and flour an 8x4x2-inch loaf pan. Pour in batter. Bake in a 350° oven 35 to 40 minutes or till done. Cool in pan 10 minutes. Remove; cool on wire rack. With knife, round off one end. If desired, level other end so cake stands straight. Wrap; refrigerate overnight.

To make this cake more stable for standing up, cover the baked cake and store in the refrigerator about 8 hours or overnight before decorating.

Cardboard
2 cups creamy white frosting *(use Butter Frosting on page 88 or a creamy white frosting mix for a 2-layer cake)*
Orange paste food coloring
Blue paste food coloring
2 cups coconut
Few drops water
Few drops yellow liquid food coloring

● Cut feet out of cardboard as shown in diagram, right. Tint ⅓ cup frosting with orange food coloring and 2 tablespoons frosting with blue food coloring. Frost top of feet with orange-tinted frosting. Stand cake on feet, rounded side up, building up orange frosting to support cake. Let stand 1 hour or till frosting is firm. Shield feet with waxed paper. Frost entire cake with untinted frosting. In screw-top jar shake together coconut, water, and liquid food coloring; press onto cake. Remove waxed paper.

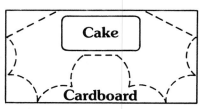

Make the feet from a piece of cardboard that's 10 inches long and 5 inches wide.

Pointed ice cream cone
2 semisweet chocolate pieces
1 vanilla wafer
1 round sugar cookie
Ribbons

● Trim cone to 3 inches. Attach cone for beak and chocolate pieces for eyes. For hat, attach vanilla wafer atop sugar cookie with the blue-tinted frosting so frosting shows. Attach to cake with frosting, securing ribbons under hat. Makes 6 servings.

South Pole Penguin: *(pictured on page 77)* Prepare cake and frosting as directed for Easter Chick. Divide and tint frosting as follows: tint ¾ cup with *black paste food coloring,* tint ½ cup with *orange paste food coloring,* and leave ¾ cup untinted. Frost top surface of cake with some untinted frosting. Spread on black-tinted frosting for wings. Spread 1 tablespoon of the orange-tinted frosting in a triangle for the beak. Add miniature *semisweet chocolate pieces* for eyes. Roll out a large *black gumdrop;* cut out bow tie shape and attach to cake. Cut feet from *cardboard* and frost tops with remaining orange-tinted frosting. Stand cake upright on feet, building up frosting to support cake. Let stand 1 hour. Reserve 2 tablespoons of the black-tinted frosting; spread remaining onto lower ⅔ of cake sides and back. Frost remaining cake with the remaining untinted frosting. For hat, attach a large *marshmallow* to a flat *chocolate cookie* with frosting. Frost with reserved black-tinted frosting, leaving a band of white at base of marshmallow for the hat band.

Colored Easter Egg: Prepare cake and frosting as directed for Easter Chick, *except* place cake top side down and round off edges to resemble an egg. Reserve ½ cup frosting. Frost cake with remaining frosting. Divide and tint the reserved frosting with desired *paste food coloring;* pipe on desired decorations with *writing tip, star tip, leaf tip, and decorating bag.*

Begin the igloo by lining the mixing bowl with a layer of cake slices.

Fill the bowl with *half* of the ice cream, a layer of cake slices, the remaining ice cream, and another layer of cake slices, reserving one cake slice for the door. Cover and freeze cake and reserved slice.

Unmold the cake by inverting the bowl onto a serving plate, holding a warm, damp towel around the bottom of the bowl about 1 minute, and then lifting the bowl.

Frost with whipped cream. Halve the reserved cake slice crosswise; stack halves next to igloo for door and frost. Score the igloo with a knife. Freeze till serving time.

Ice Cream Igloo

Batter for Chocolate Jelly Roll Cake *(see recipe, page 94)*	● Grease and lightly flour a 15x10x1-inch jelly roll pan. Spread batter evenly into prepared pan. Bake in a 375° oven for 12 to 15 minutes or till cake springs back when lightly touched.
Sifted powdered sugar	● Immediately loosen the edges of cake from pan and turn out onto a towel sprinkled with sifted powdered sugar. Starting with narrow end, roll warm cake and the towel together; cool.
½ **gallon ice cream (any flavor)**	● Soften 2 cups of the ice cream. Unroll cake; spread the softened ice cream over surface of cake to within ½ inch of edges. Roll up cake and ice cream only; wrap and freeze at least 3 hours. Soften remaining ice cream. Cut cake roll crosswise into ½-inch-thick slices. Reserve one cake slice for door; wrap and freeze. Line bottom and sides of a chilled 2½-quart mixing bowl with one layer of cake slices. Pack half of the remaining softened ice cream into the bottom of the cake-lined bowl. Top ice cream with another single layer of cake slices. Spread remaining ice cream over cake and top with a final layer of cake slices. Cover; freeze 3 hours or till firm.
1 **cup whipping cream**	● Beat whipping cream till soft peaks form. To unmold cake, invert bowl onto a serving plate and hold a warm, damp towel around the bottom of the bowl about 1 minute. Lift bowl. Reserve ¼ cup of the whipped cream for door. Frost cake with the remaining whipped cream. Halve reserved cake slice crosswise. Place halves, flat sides together, against igloo for door. Frost with the reserved whipped cream. Draw a table knife through whipped cream from top to bottom and around sides for brick effect. Freeze 1 hour or till serving time. To serve, slice into wedges. Makes 12 to 16 servings.

This *South Pole Penguin* belongs back on page 74 (with his recipe), but insisted on being photographed in his natural habitat.

Americake

Large piece of cardboard (at least 15x10 inches)	● To transfer design, draw a 15x10-inch rectangle onto a large piece of cardboard. Divide rectangle into 24 squares by drawing horizontal and vertical lines 2½ inches apart. Working several squares at a time, mark your large grid exactly where the outline of the continent intersects each line on our grid, opposite. Connect the marks on your large grid with a continuous line, following outline on our grid. Continue till entire design is made. Cut out the design. Follow the directions, right, for making the foil baking pan.	

After you've cut the design out of the cardboard, cover it with foil. Tear off about four more sheets of foil that are 12 inches wide and 16 inches long. Fold each in half crosswise to 12x8 inches, then again to 12x4 inches, then a third time to make 12x2-inch strips. Snip or tear ½-inch-long notches on one side of each strip at 1-inch intervals.

Folding notched edges under cardboard base, fit strips along the cardboard so the foil extends upward 1½ inches. Tape the strips of foil to the underside of the cardboard base and to each other as you go.

Batter for a 2-layer-size cake *(use a recipe on pages 90-92 or a 2-layer-size cake mix)*	● Grease and flour bottom and sides of foil pan. Place in a 15x10x1-inch baking pan. Pour batter into foil pan and bake in a 350° oven about 30 minutes or till a toothpick inserted in center comes out clean. Cool on wire rack. Remove foil strips, leaving cake on cardboard base.
2 cups creamy white frosting *(use Butter Frosting on page 88 or a creamy white frosting mix for a 2-layer cake)* **1 tube red decorator icing and plastic ribbon tip** **Fresh blueberries**	● Frost sides and top of cake. With a toothpick, mark a box in upper left corner of cake. With red decorator icing and ribbon tip, make stripes across top and down sides of cake, avoiding marked corner of cake. Place rows of blueberries in marked corner of cake. Makes 12 servings.

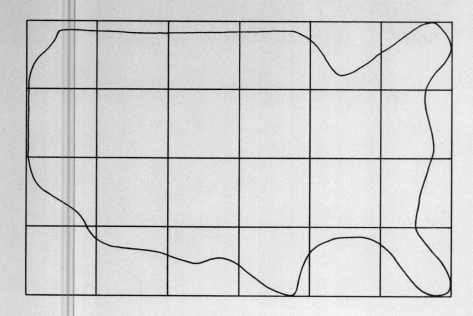

Instead of spending money on a shaped pan you'll use once in a blue moon, make your own disposable foil pan for an *Americake* using the instructions we've given you. With a little American ingenuity, you can custom-make almost any shape of pan and create other unique cake shapes.

Hidden Vegetable Garden

1 frozen chocolate loaf pound cake

● For parsnip and carrot, use a long-bladed knife to cut two wedge-shaped grooves about ½ inch wide at top and about 1 inch deep through length of cake. For radish, use a straw to hollow out a ½-inch-diameter groove through length of cake at top surface.

2 cups creamy white frosting *(use Butter Frosting on page 88 or a creamy white frosting mix for a 2-layer cake)*
Green paste food coloring
Orange paste food coloring
Red paste food coloring
Writing tip
Decorating bag *(see parchment cone on page 86 or use a pastry bag)*

● Divide and tint the frosting as follows: tint ⅓ cup with green food coloring, tint ¼ cup with orange food coloring, tint 2 tablespoons with red food coloring, and leave the remaining frosting untinted. With writing tip and decorating bag, fill in parsnip groove with ¼ cup of the untinted frosting, radish groove with the red-tinted frosting, and carrot groove with the orange-tinted frosting.

3 tablespoons unsweetened cocoa powder
Water
Leaf tip

● Combine remaining 1 cup untinted frosting and cocoa powder. Stir in enough water (about 1 teaspoon) to make of spreading consistency; frost top and long sides of cake, reserving some for ends. Use leaf tip to pipe green-tinted frosting in rows above vegetables for green tops. Frost ends with remaining chocolate frosting. Chill. To serve, slice crosswise. Makes 8 servings.

Hiking Boot Surprise: On bottom of a frozen *chocolate loaf pound cake*, cut four grooves ¼ inch wide and ¼ inch deep through length of cake for treads. Make a vertical cut ½ inch deep down middle of cake top. Make a horizontal cut into one long side of cake ¼ inch from top edge, slicing into cake to meet cut from top. Remove section of cake. Round the corner off outer cut edge for toe of boot. For laces, cut grooves into cut surface of cake, making grooves ⅛ inch wide and ½ inch deep. Divide and tint 2 cups *creamy white frosting* as follows: tint ½ cup with *yellow paste food coloring*, ½ cup with *black paste food coloring*, and combine remaining 1 cup with 3 tablespoons *unsweetened cocoa powder* and enough *water* (about 1 teaspoon) to make of spreading consistency. With a *writing tip* and *decorating bag*, pipe yellow-tinted frosting into lace grooves and black-tinted frosting into tread grooves, filling all air spaces. Place cake tread side down. Frost all exposed surfaces with the chocolate frosting. If desired, pipe remaining yellow-tinted frosting on cake where boot would tie. Chill. To serve, slice crosswise. Serves 8.

Car in the Garage: On bottom of a frozen *plain loaf pound cake*, use the tip of a vegetable peeler to hollow out two 1-inch-diameter grooves through length of cake for wheels. Make a vertical cut ¾ inch deep down middle of cake top. Make a horizontal cut into one long side of cake ½ inch from top edge, slicing into cake to meet cut from top. Remove section of cake. Divide and tint 2 cups *creamy white frosting* as follows: tint 1 cup with *green paste food coloring*, 2 tablespoons with *red paste food coloring*, leave 2 tablespoons untinted, and combine remaining ¾ cup with 2 tablespoons *unsweetened cocoa powder* and enough water (about ½ teaspoon) to make of spreading consistency. Spread chocolate frosting into wheel grooves, pushing out any air bubbles. Place cake with wheels side down. Frost all exposed surfaces with the green-tinted frosting. With a *ribbon tip or writing tip* and *decorating bag,* pipe a stripe of untinted frosting along side of cake just below cut edge for headlight. Use a *writing tip* to pipe the red-tinted frosting ᵗᵒ side of cake ½ inch

These cakes are nothing special to look at—that is until you slice them. When you do, you'll see a design in the cross-section of each piece.

Greasing and Flouring Pans

Keep cakes from sticking to pans by greasing and lightly flouring the pans before pouring in the batter. To grease, use folded paper toweling or waxed paper to generously apply shortening to the bottom and sides of the pan (about 1 tablespoon shortening for an 8- or 9-inch round or square baking pan and about 2 tablespoons for a 13x9- or 15x10-inch baking pan). Sprinkle flour into the greased pan (about 2 teaspoons for an 8- or 9-inch round or square pan and 4 teaspoons for a 13x9- or 15x10-inch pan). Tilt and tap the pan to distribute the flour evenly. Tap out excess flour.

Pan-coat greasing is the one-step way to grease and flour a pan. You can purchase an aerosol pan-coating product or make your own from items on your pantry shelf. To make your own pan-coating, follow the instructions, right.

To make your own pan-coating, stir together ⅔ cup *shortening* and ⅓ cup *all-purpose flour* till well mixed. To use, generously spread the mixture on the bottom and sides of the pan (about 1½ tablespoons for an 8-inch or 9-inch baking pan and 3 tablespoons for a 13x9-inch or 15x10-inch baking pan). There will be enough mixture to coat eight small pans or four large pans. Store the extra pan-coating in a covered container in the cupboard.

Removing Cakes from Pans

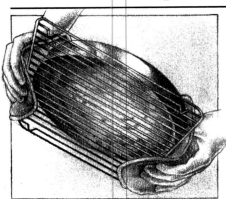

After removing a cake from the oven, let it cool in the pan on a wire rack about 10 minutes. If the cake is cooled in the pan much longer than 10 minutes, it may be difficult to get out. Remove the cake from the pan by placing a wire rack upside down over the cake and inverting the cake onto the rack. Lift off the pan.

Because the top of a cake is slightly rounded, the inverted cake won't rest securely on the rack. This could cause a warm, tender cake to crack. To prevent this cracking, place a second wire rack atop the inverted cake and flip it over so the base rests on the rack. Lift off the top rack. Cool the cake thoroughly before frosting it.

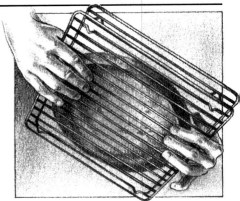

Getting Ready to Frost

Leveling

Leveling: A cake with a rounded top will not rest securely on a plate or provide a flat top surface for decorating. If this is a problem with your cake, slice off the rounded part with a long-bladed serrated knife using a back-and-forth sawing motion. This will be easier to do if the cake is partially frozen.

Crumbing: Loose crumbs are a cake decorator's enemy because they get into the frosting and mar the appearance of the cake. Get rid of excess crumbs on a cake before you frost it by brushing them away with a pastry brush or your hand.

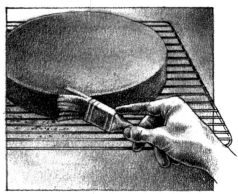

Crumbing

When the cake design doesn't depend on the shape of cake, you can substitute pans using this chart as a guide. Interchange any of the pans in the left column and bake in a 350° oven for times given in the right column. (Baking times are based on 5 to 6 cups of batter.)

Baking Pan Substitutions

Pan Equivalents	Baking Time (350°)
Two 8x1½-inch or 9x1½-inch round baking pans	25 to 35 minutes
Two 8x8x2-inch baking pans	25 to 35 minutes
One 13x9x2-inch baking pan	30 to 35 minutes
One 15x10x1-inch baking pan	25 to 30 minutes

Assembling a Layer Cake

Place the first cake layer, top side down, on a serving plate (unless specified otherwise for a particular cake). Tuck several strips of waxed paper just under the edge of the cake to keep the serving plate from getting smeared with frosting while you decorate.

Spread about ½ cup of frosting over this first layer with a metal spatula. When using a firm, creamy frosting such as Butter Frosting, spread the frosting to the edge of the cake. When using a soft frosting such as Fluffy White Frosting, leave about ¼ inch unfrosted around the edge of the layer. The weight of the second cake layer will cause the fluffy frosting to flow to the edge. Place the second cake layer, top side up, over the frosted layer. Make sure the edges of the cake layers align.

Be sure you tuck the strips of waxed paper just under the edge of the cake so you can remove them easily when you're finished frosting the cake.

Icing and Frosting

Icing: To seal any crumbs still clinging to the cake or to seal the cut edges of cut-up cakes, you may want to ice the cake with a coat of frosting you have thinned with water. Stir enough water into a small amount of frosting to make it the consistency of sour cream. Spread the sides or cut edges of the cake with just enough icing to coat.

Frosting: Starting with the sides, spread frosting on the cake, smoothing the frosting with the edge of a metal spatula held upright against the side of the cake. Now spread the top of the cake with frosting to meet the frosting on the sides, keeping the spatula almost parallel to the top surface of the cake. Smooth with the edge of the metal spatula.

If adding a bottom border, remove the waxed paper strips before piping. Otherwise, remove strips before serving.

For an extra smooth look on cakes frosted with a creamy frosting such as Butter Frosting, dip a metal spatula in hot water, shake off the excess water droplets, and smooth the sides and top of the cake with the spatula.

Types of Frosting

Creamy Frosting

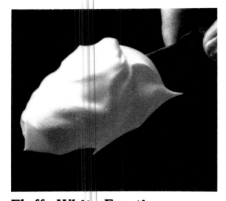

Fluffy White Frosting

Creamy Frostings (such as Butter Frosting, Chocolate Butter Frosting, Cream Cheese Frosting, Pure White Creamy Frosting, and packaged creamy white and creamy chocolate frosting mixes) are ideal for decorating cakes because they have a smooth consistency and spread easily, yet are firm enough for piping decorations. Another plus is that they can be stored in a tightly covered container in the refrigerator 1 week or in the freezer 6 months.

Creamy white frosting mix and the recipes for Butter Frosting (page 88) and Cream Cheese Frosting (page 89) make slightly off-white frostings. To frost a cake with a pure white frosting, such as a wedding cake, use the recipe for Pure White Creamy Frosting (page 89).

In this book, feel free to substitute a creamy white frosting mix for Butter Frosting or a creamy chocolate frosting mix for Chocolate Butter Frosting. Canned frosting is not generally recommended for frosting cakes to be decorated since it is softer and makes applying decorations difficult.

Fluffy White Frosting (page 88) spreads easily, and has a fluffy consistency and a glossy appearance. Use immediately. Do not freeze.

Royal Icing (page 89) is a smooth icing that dries candy-hard. It can be spread on cakes as well as used for piping decorations. Since it dries very fast, you'll need to work quickly. Do not freeze.

If you are making a creamy frosting mix to use only for piping on decorations, prepare the mix according to package directions, *except* omit the butter or margarine. This will produce a firmer frosting for a well-defined piping decoration.

Coloring Frosting

Paste food coloring is recommended over liquid food coloring because it tints frosting without thinning it. Purchase it at cake decorating stores, at some supermarkets, or from mail order catalogs.

Because paste food coloring is highly concentrated, start out with a small amount and add more as needed. Use the tip of a toothpick to add small amounts to the frosting. Mix it in thoroughly before adding more coloring.

Decorating Bags

Rolled parchment cone

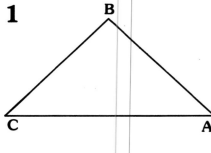

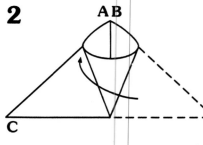

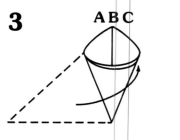

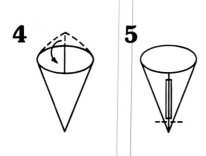

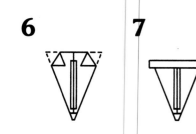

Choose the type of decorating bag that is easiest for you to use. Decorating bags made of plastic-coated cloth or a synthetic material are reusable but must be washed and dried each time you change frosting color. Purchase them at department stores, craft shops, or from mail order firms. Cake decorating kits are available (some grocers carry them) that provide a decorating bag as well as decorating tips, plastic couplers, and instructions.

You can make your own disposable decorating bags from parchment that you purchase at a craft shop or grocer. These eliminate messy cleanup because you make a different cone for each frosting color and throw the cones away when you're finished decorating. Here are two ways to make them:

Rolled parchment cone: Hold a 12x12x17-inch parchment triangle with the long side at the bottom. Curl the lower right corner (A) over to point (B) to form a cone. Hold points (A) and (B) together with your right hand. Bring corner (C) around the front of the cone so points (A), (B), and (C) meet and there is no opening at the tip. Fold the points down into the cone. Tape the outside seam to about 1 inch from the tip. With scissors, snip off ½ to ¾ inch from the tip, depending on the decorating tip you'll be using. Drop desired decorating tip into the cone. Half-fill the cone with frosting, using a knife or metal spatula. Fold in top corners, then fold top down to meet the frosting level.

Folded parchment cone: Fold a 10x6-inch parchment rectangle in half crosswise. Unfold; fold corner (A) in to meet center crease. Fold the left half of the rectangle over the right half and fold corner (B) up to left folded edge. Insert hand into cone to open; tape the outside seam to about 1 inch from tip. Fold points down into cone. Snip, insert tip, fill, and fold down top as directed for rolled cone.

Shortcut cone: For small jobs requiring no decorating tip, you can use a heavy plastic sandwich bag or an envelope for a decorating bag. Half-fill the bag or envelope with frosting, seal, and snip the point off one of the corners with scissors. Use for writing messages, making dots, or drawing lines.

Folded parchment cone

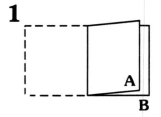

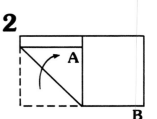

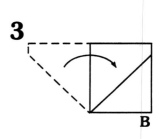

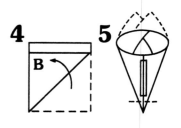

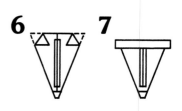

Using Decorating Bag and Tips

Hand position

Hand position: To hold the decorating bag, place the full end in the palm of your writing hand and force the frosting toward the tip by squeezing your hand together. Use your other hand to guide the tip of the bag. With practice, you will learn to control the flow of the frosting by regulating the pressure.

Writing tip: This tip has a simple round opening for making dots and lines and for writing. For dots, hold the bag at a 90-degree angle (straight up and down) with the tip almost touching the cake. Squeeze out a dot of frosting the size you want. Stop the pressure, then lift off. To make lines and write, hold the bag at a 45-degree angle. Guiding the tip just above the cake with your free hand, squeeze with your writing hand. To end each letter, gently touch the tip to the cake, release pressure, then lift off.

Leaf tip: Use this tip at a 45-degree angle to make leaves, ruffles, and stripes. For leaves, with the point just above the cake, squeeze out some frosting to make the base of the leaf. Continue squeezing but ease up on the pressure as you pull away. Stop the pressure, then lift off. For curly leaves, wiggle your hand as you squeeze. For ruffles, touch tip to cake and move up and down as you squeeze. For stripes, touch tip to cake and apply even pressure as you pull away.

Star tip: Make stars, rosettes, shells, and zigzags with this tip. For stars, hold the bag at a 90-degree angle with the tip just above the cake. Squeeze out some frosting, stop pressure, then lift off. For rosettes, hold the bag at a 90-degree angle. Squeeze out some frosting as for a star. As you continue to squeeze, move the tip slightly to the left, then up and around in a clockwise direction till you arrive back at the starting point. Stop pressure and pull away. For shells, hold the bag at a 45-degree angle. With tip just above cake, squeeze out some frosting till you've formed a full mound; ease up on the pressure and pull the tip down till it touches the cake. Stop pressure and pull away. Start the next shell at the stopping point of the previous one (shells will overlap slightly). For zigzags, hold the bag at a 45-degree angle. Touch tip to cake and move from side to side as you squeeze.

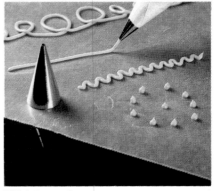

**Writing tip
(tip numbers 2-4)**

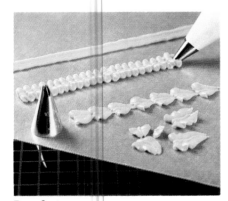

**Leaf tip
(tip numbers 66-70)**

**Star tip
(tip numbers 17 and 18)**

Butter Frosting

2 CUPS		1 CUP
6 tablespoons butter *or* margarine 4½ to 4¾ cups sifted powdered sugar	● In small mixer bowl beat butter or margarine till light and fluffy. Gradually add about half of the powdered sugar, beating well.	3 tablespoons butter *or* margarine 2¼ to 2½ cups sifted powdered sugar
¼ cup milk 1½ teaspoons vanilla	● Beat in milk and vanilla. Gradually beat in remaining powdered sugar; beat in additional milk, if necessary, to make frosting of spreading consistency.	2 tablespoons milk ¾ teaspoon vanilla

Chocolate Butter Frosting

2 CUPS		1 CUP
2 squares (2 ounces) unsweetened chocolate 6 tablespoons butter *or* margarine 4½ to 4¾ cups sifted powdered sugar	● In a saucepan melt unsweetened chocolate over low heat, stirring frequently; cool. In small mixer bowl beat butter or margarine till light and fluffy. Gradually add about half of the powdered sugar, beating well.	1 square (1 ounce) unsweetened chocolate 3 tablespoons butter *or* margarine 2¼ to 2½ cups sifted powdered sugar
¼ cup milk 1½ teaspoons vanilla	● Beat in milk, vanilla, and cooled, melted chocolate. Gradually beat in remaining powdered sugar; beat in additional milk, if necessary, to make frosting of spreading consistency.	2 tablespoons milk ¾ teaspoon vanilla

Fluffy White Frosting

5 CUPS		2½ CUPS
1 cup sugar ⅓ cup water ¼ teaspoon cream of tartar Dash salt	● In a saucepan combine the sugar, water, cream of tartar, and salt. Cook and stir till the mixture is bubbly and sugar is dissolved.	½ cup sugar 3 tablespoons water ⅛ teaspoon cream of tartar Dash salt
2 egg whites 1 teaspoon vanilla	● In a mixer bowl combine egg white(s) and vanilla. Add the sugar mixture very slowly to the unbeaten egg white(s) while beating constantly with electric mixer on high speed about 7 minutes or till stiff peaks form.	1 egg white ½ teaspoon vanilla

Frosting Amounts for Basic Shapes

When using these frosting recipes with ingredients listed on the left and right sides, keep in mind that amounts on the left will frost the tops and sides of two 8- or 9-inch layers, the top and sides of a 13x9-inch cake, or 24 cupcakes. Amounts on the right will frost the top of a 13x9-inch cake, top and sides of one 8- or 9-inch round layer or 8-inch square cake, or 12 cupcakes.

Cream Cheese Frosting

2⅔ CUPS		1⅓ CUPS
2 3-ounce packages cream cheese ½ cup butter *or* margarine 2 teaspoons vanilla	● In a mixer bowl beat together the cream cheese, butter or margarine, and vanilla till light and fluffy.	1 3-ounce package cream cheese ¼ cup butter *or* margarine 1 teaspoon vanilla
4 cups sifted powdered sugar	● Gradually add the powdered sugar, beating till smooth.	2 cups sifted powdered sugar

Pure White Creamy Frosting

2½ cups white shortening 1¼ teaspoons almond extract	● In large mixer bowl beat shortening and almond extract with electric mixer on medium speed about 30 seconds.
11½ to 12 cups sifted powdered sugar (2½ pounds) ½ cup to ⅔ cup milk	● Gradually add about half of the powdered sugar, beating well. Add ⅓ *cup* of the milk. Gradually beat in remaining powdered sugar and enough of the remaining milk to make of spreading consistency. Makes 7½ cups.

Royal Icing

3 egg whites 1 16-ounce package powdered sugar, sifted (about 4¾ cups) 1 teaspoon vanilla ½ teaspoon cream of tartar	● In large mixer bowl combine egg whites, powdered sugar, vanilla, and cream of tartar. Beat with electric mixer on high speed for 7 to 10 minutes or till very stiff. Use at once, covering icing in bowl at all times with wet paper toweling to prevent drying. Makes 3 cups.

Yellow Cake

2-LAYER-SIZE CAKE		1-LAYER-SIZE CAKE
2¾ cups all-purpose flour 2½ teaspoons baking powder 1 teaspoon salt	● Grease and lightly flour baking pan(s). For 2-layer-size cake, use two 8x1½-inch *or* 9x1½-inch round baking pans *or* one 13x9x2-inch baking pan. For 1-layer-size cake, use one 8x1½-inch *or* 9x1½-inch round baking pan *or* one 8x8x2-inch baking pan. In a bowl stir together the flour, baking powder, and salt.	1⅓ cups all-purpose flour 1¼ teaspoons baking powder ½ teaspoon salt
½ cup butter *or* margarine 1¾ cups sugar 1½ teaspoons vanilla	● In a mixer bowl beat butter or margarine with electric mixer on medium speed about 30 seconds. Add sugar and vanilla; beat till well combined.	¼ cup butter *or* margarine ¾ cup sugar ¾ teaspoon vanilla
2 eggs 1¼ cups milk	● Add egg(s) one at a time, beating 1 minute after each. Add flour mixture and milk alternately to beaten mixture, beating on low speed after each addition just till combined. Turn into pan(s). Bake in a 350° oven 30 to 35 minutes for all cake sizes or till a toothpick inserted in center comes out clean. Cool 10 minutes in pan(s) on wire rack(s). Remove if desired; cool completely. A 2-layer-size cake makes 12 servings; a 1-layer-size cake makes 6 servings. **Yellow Cupcakes:** Grease and lightly flour muffin pans or line with paper bake cups. Prepare Yellow Cake batter as above. Fill each cup half full. Bake in a 350° oven about 20 minutes or till done. Cool 5 minutes in pans on wire rack. Remove; cool completely. A 2-layer-size cake makes about 24; a 1-layer-size cake makes about 12.	1 egg ⅔ cup milk

White Cake

2-LAYER-SIZE CAKE		1-LAYER-SIZE CAKE

2-LAYER-SIZE CAKE		1-LAYER-SIZE CAKE
2 cups all-purpose flour 1½ cups sugar 1 tablespoon baking powder 1 teaspoon salt	● Grease and lightly flour baking pan(s). For 2-layer-size cake, use two 8x1½-inch or 9x1½-inch round baking pans or one 13x9x2-inch baking pan. For 1-layer-size cake, use one 8x1½-inch or 9x1½-inch round baking pan or one 8x8x2-inch baking pan. 　　In a mixer bowl stir together flour, sugar, baking powder, and salt.	1 cup all-purpose flour ¾ cup sugar 1½ teaspoons baking powder ½ teaspoon salt
1 cup milk ½ cup shortening 2 teaspoons vanilla	● Add milk, shortening, and vanilla to the flour mixture; beat with electric mixer on low speed till combined. Beat on medium speed for 2 minutes.	½ cup milk ¼ cup shortening 1 teaspoon vanilla
4 egg whites	● Add unbeaten egg whites; beat on medium speed 2 minutes more, scraping sides of bowl frequently. Turn into prepared pan(s); spread evenly. 　　Bake in a 350° oven 25 to 30 minutes for all cake sizes or till a toothpick inserted in center comes out clean. Cool 10 minutes in pan(s) on wire rack(s). Remove if desired; cool completely. A 2-layer-size cake makes 12 servings; a 1-layer-size cake makes 6 servings.	2 egg whites

Carrot Cake

2-LAYER-SIZE CAKE		1-LAYER-SIZE CAKE
2 cups all-purpose flour 2 cups sugar 1 teaspoon baking powder 1 teaspoon baking soda 1 teaspoon salt 1 teaspoon ground cinnamon	● Grease and lightly flour baking pan(s). For 2-layer-size cake, use two 8x1½-inch or 9x1½-inch round baking pans or one 13x9x2-inch baking pan. For 1-layer-size cake, use one 8x1½-inch or 9x1½-inch round baking pan or one 8x8x2-inch baking pan. 　　In a mixer bowl stir together flour, sugar, baking powder, baking soda, salt, and cinnamon.	1 cup all-purpose flour 1 cup sugar ½ teaspoon baking powder ½ teaspoon baking soda ½ teaspoon salt ½ teaspoon ground cinnamon
3 cups finely shredded carrot 1 cup cooking oil 4 eggs	● Add carrot, cooking oil, and eggs; beat with electric mixer on low speed till combined. Beat on medium speed for 2 minutes. Turn into prepared pan(s). 　　Bake in a 325° oven till a toothpick inserted in center comes out clean: 40 minutes for 8- or 9-inch round layer(s) or 8-inch square cake and 50 to 60 minutes for 13x9-inch cake. Cool 10 minutes in pan(s) on wire rack(s). Remove if desired; cool completely. A 2-layer-size cake makes 12 to 15 servings; a 1-layer-size cake makes 6 to 8 servings.	1½ cups finely shredded carrot ½ cup cooking oil 2 eggs

Chocolate Cake

2-LAYER-SIZE CAKE

1-LAYER-SIZE CAKE

2-LAYER-SIZE CAKE		1-LAYER-SIZE CAKE
2 cups all-purpose flour **2 cups sugar** **1 teaspoon baking soda** **½ teaspoon salt**	● Grease and lightly flour baking pan(s). For 2-layer-size cake, use two 8x1½-inch *or* 9x1½-inch round baking pans, one 15x10x1-inch baking pan, *or* one 13x9x2-inch baking pan. For 1-layer-size cake, use one 8x1½-inch *or* 9x1½-inch round baking pan *or* one 8x8x2-inch baking pan. In a mixer bowl stir together flour, sugar, baking soda, and salt.	**1 cup all-purpose flour** **1 cup sugar** **½ teaspoon baking soda** **¼ teaspoon salt**

1 cup butter *or* margarine
1 cup water
⅓ cup unsweetened cocoa
     powder
	● In a saucepan combine butter or margarine, water, and cocoa powder. Bring just to boiling, stirring constantly. Remove from heat. Add cocoa mixture to flour mixture; beat with electric mixer on low speed just till combined.	**½ cup butter *or* margarine**
		½ cup water
		3 tablespoons
		     unsweetened cocoa
		     powder

2 eggs
½ cup buttermilk
     or sour milk
1½ teaspoons vanilla
	● Add egg(s), buttermilk or sour milk, and vanilla; beat on low speed 1 minute. (Batter will be thin.) Turn batter into prepared pan(s).
	    Bake in a 350° oven till a toothpick inserted in center comes out clean: 25 to 30 minutes for 8- or 9-inch round layer(s), 8-inch square cake, or 15x10-inch cake, and 30 to 35 minutes for 13x9-inch cake. Cool 10 minutes in pan(s) on wire rack(s). Remove if desired; cool completely. A 2-layer-size cake makes 12 to 15 servings; a 1-layer-size cake makes 6 to 8 servings.
		1 egg
		¼ cup buttermilk
		     or sour milk
		¾ teaspoon vanilla

Hot Milk Sponge Cake Batter

1 RECIPE		½ RECIPE

1 cup all-purpose flour
**1 teaspoon baking
   powder**
¼ teaspoon salt
	● In a bowl stir together the flour, baking powder, and salt.	**½ cup all-purpose flour**
		**½ teaspoon baking
		   powder**
		⅛ teaspoon salt

2 eggs **1 cup sugar**	● In small mixer bowl beat egg(s) with electric mixer on high speed about 4 minutes or till thick. Gradually add sugar; beat on medium speed about 4 minutes more or till sugar dissolves, scraping bottom and sides of bowl occasionally. Add flour mixture to egg mixture; stir just till blended.	**1 egg** **½ cup sugar**

½ cup milk
**2 tablespoons butter *or*
   margarine**
	● In a saucepan heat milk with butter or margarine till butter melts. Stir into batter and mix well. Pour into pan specified in recipe and bake in a 350° oven for designated amount of time. One recipe makes 9 servings; ½ recipe makes 4 or 5 servings.
	Note: For cakes other than those in this book, 1 recipe Hot Milk Sponge Cake Batter may be baked in a greased and floured 9x9x2-inch baking pan in a 350° oven for 20 to 25 minutes; ½ recipe Hot Milk Sponge Cake Batter may be baked in a greased and floured 9x5x3-inch loaf pan in a 350° oven for 18 to 20 minutes.
		¼ cup milk
		**1 tablespoon butter *or*
		   margarine**

Jelly Roll Cake

½ cup all-purpose flour 1 teaspoon baking powder ¼ teaspoon salt	● Grease and lightly flour a 15x10x1-inch jelly roll pan. In a bowl stir together flour, baking powder, and salt.
4 egg yolks ½ teaspoon vanilla ⅓ cup sugar	● In small mixer bowl beat egg yolks and vanilla with electric mixer on high speed about 5 minutes or till thick and lemon colored. Gradually add the ⅓ cup sugar, beating till sugar dissolves. Thoroughly wash beaters.
4 egg whites ½ cup sugar	● In large mixer bowl beat egg whites with electric mixer on medium speed till soft peaks form. Gradually add the ½ cup sugar; continue beating till stiff peaks form. Fold yolk mixture into egg whites.
Sifted powdered sugar	● Sprinkle flour mixture over egg mixture; fold in lightly by hand. Spread batter evenly in prepared pan. Bake in a 375° oven for 12 to 15 minutes or till cake springs back and leaves no imprint when lightly touched. Immediately loosen edges of cake from pan and turn out onto a towel sprinkled with sifted powdered sugar. Starting with narrow end, roll warm cake and towel together; cool on a wire rack.
½ cup jelly *or* jam	● Unroll cake; spread with jelly or jam to within 1 inch of edges. Roll up cake. Makes 10 servings.

Chocolate Jelly Roll Cake: **Prepare Jelly Roll Cake, *except* sift ¼ cup unsweetened *cocoa powder* together with flour mixture.**

Index